Mindful Mandala Afghans

Mandalas are not just for coloring books! With our easy patterns you can create artful afghans that will be showpieces in any room in your home.

The Lion Brand Design team has stepped out of the box, literally, to create an exciting collection of 10 afghans that incorporate the dozens of vibrant colors of Vanna's Choice® Yarn. Vanna's Choice is a 100% acrylic premium easy care yarn, so your afghans will be soft, cozy and easy care.

The best part is that a portion of your purchase of Vanna's Choice will go to St. Jude Children's Hospital. With your help, Lion Brand and Vanna White have already donated over $1.7 Million to St Jude.

So put down your coloring book, pick up your crochet hook and start stitching.

I0877492

About Lion Brand® Yarn Company

Lion Brand® Yarn Company is a 5th generation, family-owned and operated business, and a beloved American brand since 1878. The company is devoted to inspiring and educating knitters and crocheters with yarns, patterns, how-tos, and ideas that elevate their yarn crafting experience.

LEISURE ARTS, INC. • Maumelle, Arkansas

Circle of Flowers Mandala Afghan

INTERMEDIATE

SIZE

About 50" (127 cm) diameter

Shopping List

Yarn (Medium Weight) MEDIUM 4

LION BRAND® VANNA'S CHOICE® (Art. #860)

- ☐ #158 Mustard - 1 ball (A)
- ☐ #112 Raspberry - 1 ball (B)
- ☐ #301 Rose Mist - 1 ball (C)
- ☐ #098 Fisherman - 1 ball (D)
- ☐ #101 Pink - 1 ball (E)
- ☐ #171 Fern - 1 ball (F)
- ☐ #176 Peacock - 1 ball (G)
- ☐ #108 Dusty Blue - 1 ball (H)
- ☐ #111 Sky Blue - 1 ball (I)
- ☐ #109 Colonial Blue - 1 ball (J)

or colors of your choice

Crochet Hook

LION BRAND® crochet hook

- ☐ Size J-10 (6 mm)

or size needed for gauge

Additional Supplies

- ☐ LION BRAND® stitch markers
- ☐ LION BRAND® large-eyed blunt needle

GAUGE

Rnds 1-6 of Center Flower = about 7½" (19 cm) diameter.

BE SURE TO CHECK YOUR GAUGE.

STITCH GUIDE

BEGINNING 2 DOUBLE CROCHET CLUSTER (abbreviated beg 2-dc Cl)

Ch 3, yarn over, insert hook in indicated st and draw up a loop, yarn over and draw through 2 loops on hook (2 loops rem on hook); yarn over and draw through rem 2 loops on hook.

2 DOUBLE CROCHET CLUSTER (abbreviated 2-dc Cl)

Yarn over, insert hook in indicated st and draw up a loop, yarn over and draw through 2 loops on hook (2 loops rem on hook), yarn over, insert hook in *same* st and draw up a loop, yarn over and draw through 2 loops on hook, yarn over and draw through all 3 loops on hook.

BEGINNING 3 DOUBLE CROCHET CLUSTER (abbreviated beg 3-dc Cl)

Ch 3, yarn over, insert hook in indicated st and draw up a loop, yarn over and draw through 2 loops on hook (2 loops rem on hook); yarn over, insert hook in *same* st and draw up a loop, yarn over and draw through 2 loops on hook, yarn over and draw through all 3 loops on hook.

3 DOUBLE CROCHET CLUSTER (abbreviated 3-dc Cl)

Yarn over, insert hook in indicated st, yarn over and draw up a loop, yarn over and draw through 2 loops on hook (2 loops rem on hook), (yarn over, insert hook in *same* st, yarn over and draw up a loop, yarn over and draw through 2 loops on hook) twice; yarn over and draw through all 4 loops on hook.

NOTES

1. Afghan is worked in sections: Center Flower, Middle Rings, Triangle Points, and Outer Flowers.
2. Center Flower is worked in joined rnds with RS always facing. Middle Rings are worked in joined and turned rnds. 12 Triangle Points are worked back and forth in rows.
3. 12 Outer Flowers are worked separately and crocheted to Afghan.
4. A border is worked around the outside edge of the Afghan.
5. Yarn color is changed frequently to create bands of color.
6. To change yarn color, fasten off the old color and join new color as instructed.
7. Stitch diagrams are provided to clarify construction.

AFGHAN

Center Flower

Note: In this section work all rnds with the RS always facing. Do NOT turn work at beginning of rnds.

With A, ch 6; join with sl st in first ch to make a ring.

Rnd 1 (RS): Ch 3 (counts as first dc), work 11 more dc in ring; join with sl st in top of beg ch – 12 dc . Fasten off.

Rnd 2: From RS, join B with sc in any sp between sts, *ch 1, sc in next sp between sts; rep from * around, ch 1; join with sl st in first sc – 12 sc and 12 ch-1 sps. Fasten off.

Rnd 3: From RS, draw up a loop of C in any ch-1 sp, work beg 3-dc Cl in same ch-1 sp, *ch 2, 3-dc Cl in next ch-1 sp; rep from * around, ch 2; join with sl st in top of beg 3-dc Cl – 12 Cl and 12 ch-2 sps. Fasten off.

Rnd 4: From RS, draw up a loop of D in any ch-2 sp, (beg 2-dc Cl, ch 1, 2-dc Cl) in same ch-2 sp, *ch 1, (2-dc Cl, ch 1, 2-dc Cl) in next ch-2 sp; rep from * around, ch 1; join with sl st in top of beg 2-dc Cl – 24 Cl and 24 ch-1 sps. Fasten off.

Rnd 5: From RS, join E with sc in any ch-1 sp, sc in same ch-1 sp, *ch 1, 2 sc in next ch-1 sp; rep from * around, ch 1; join with sl st in first sc – Twenty-four 2-sc groups and 24 ch-1 sps. Fasten off.

Rnd 6: From RS, draw up a loop of B in any ch-1 sp, ch 3 (counts as dc), 2 dc in same ch-1 sp, 3 dc in each rem ch-1 sp around; join with sl st in top of beg ch – Twenty-four 3-dc groups. Fasten off.

Rnd 7: From RS, join A with sc in any st, *ch 1, sk next st, sc in next st; rep from * to last st, ch 1, sk last st; join with sl st in first sc – 36 sc and 36 ch-1 sps. Do not fasten off.

Rnd 8: With A, (sl st, 2 sc) in first ch-1 sp, *ch 1, 2 sc in next ch-1 sp; rep from * around, ch 1; join with sl st in first sc – Thirty-six 2-sc groups and 36 ch-1 sps. Fasten off.

Rnd 9: From RS, join F with sc in first st of any 2-sc group, sc in next st, *ch 1, sk next ch-1 sp, sc in next 2 sts; rep from * to last ch-1 sp, ch 1, sk last ch-1 sp; join with sl st in first sc.

Rnd 10: With F, ch 3 (counts as first dc), dc in next st, *ch 1, sk next ch-1 sp, dc in next 2 sts; rep from * to last ch-1 sp, ch 1, sk last ch-1 sp; join with sl st in top of beg ch – Thirty-six 2-dc groups and 36 ch-1 sps. Do not fasten off.

Middle Rings

Notes:

1. In this section, turn the work at the beginning of each rnd.
2. Each rnd begins in a specific way. Be sure to read the instructions carefully for working the first st in each rnd!

Rnd 11 (WS): With F, ch 1, turn, sc in same ch as joining sl st, *ch 1, sk next ch-1 sp, sc in next 2 sts; rep from * to last ch-1 sp, ch 1, sk last ch-1 sp, sc in last st; join with sl st in first sc – Thirty-six 2-sc groups and 36 ch-1 sps. Fasten off.

Rnd 12 (RS): From RS, draw up a loop of G in first sc of any 2-sc group, ch 3 (counts as dc), dc in next st, *ch 2, sk next ch-1 sp, dc in next 2 sts; rep from * to last ch-1 sp, ch 2, sk last ch-1 sp; join with sl st in top of beg ch – Thirty-six 2-dc groups and 36 ch-2 sps.

Rnd 13: With G, ch 1, turn, sc in same ch as joining sl st, *ch 2, sk next ch-2 sp, sc in next 2 sts; rep from * to last ch-2 sp, ch 2, sk last ch-2 sp, sc in last st; join with sl st in first sc – Thirty-six 2-sc groups and 36 ch-2 sps.

Rnd 14: With G, ch 3 (counts as dc), turn, dc in first st, *ch 2, sk next ch-2 sp, dc in next 2 sts; rep from * to last ch-2 sp, ch 2, sk last ch-2 sp; join with sl st in top of beg ch – Thirty-six 2-dc groups and 36 ch-2 sps.

Rnd 15: With G, ch 1, turn, sc in same ch as joining sl st, *ch 2, sk next ch-2 sp, 2 sc in next st, sc in next st; rep from * to last ch-2 sp, ch 2, sk last ch-2 sp, 2 sc in last st; join with sl st in first sc – Thirty-six 3-sc-groups and 36 ch-2 sps.
Fasten off.

Rnd 16: From RS, draw up a loop of H in first sc of any 3-sc group, ch 3 (counts as dc), dc in next 2 sts, *ch 2, sk next ch-2 sp, dc in next 3 sts; rep from * to last ch-2 sp, ch 2, sk last ch-2 sp; join with sl st in top of beg ch – Thirty-six 3-dc groups and 36 ch-2 sps.

Rnd 17: With H, ch 1, turn, sc in same ch as joining sl st, *ch 2, sk next ch-2 sp, sc in next 3 sts; rep from * to last ch-2 sp, ch 2, sk last ch-2 sp, sc in last 2 sts; join with sl st in first sc – Thirty-six 3-sc groups and 36 ch-2 sps.

Rnd 18: With H, ch 3 (counts as dc), turn, dc in first 2 sts, *ch 2, sk next ch-2 sp, dc in next 3 sts; rep from * around, ch 2, sk last ch-2 sp; join with sl st in top of beg ch.

Rnd 19: With H, ch 1, turn, sc in same ch as joining sl st, *ch 2, sk next ch-2 sp, sc in next st, 2 sc in next st, sc in next st; rep from * to last ch-2 sp, ch 2, sk last ch-2 sp, sc in next st, 2 sc in last st; join with sl st in first sc – Thirty-six 4-sc groups and 36 ch-2 sps.

Rnd 20: With H, ch 3 (counts as dc), turn, dc in first 3 sts, *ch 2, sk next ch-2 sp, dc in next 4 sts; rep from * to last ch-2 sp, ch 2, sk last ch-2 sp; join with sl st in top of beg ch – Thirty-six 4-dc groups and 36 ch-2 sps.

Rnd 21: With H, ch 1, turn, sc in same ch as joining sl st, *ch 2, sk next ch-2 sp, sc in next 4 sts; rep from * to last ch-2 sp, ch 2, sk last ch-2 sp, sc in last 3 sts; join with sl st in first sc – Thirty-six 4-sc groups and 36 ch-2 sps. Fasten off.

Rnd 22: From RS, draw up a loop of I in first sc of any 4-sc group, ch 3 (counts as dc), dc in next 3 sts, *ch 2, sk next ch-2 sp, dc in next 4 sts; rep from * to last ch-2 sp, ch 2, sk last ch-2 sp; join with sl st in top of beg ch – Thirty-six 4-dc groups and 36 ch-2 sps.

Rnd 23: With I, rep Rnd 21.

Rnd 24: With I, rep Rnd 20.

Rnd 25: With I, ch 1, turn, sc in same ch as joining sl st, *ch 2, sk next ch-2 sp, sc in next 2 sts, ch 1, sc in next 2 sts; rep from * to last ch-2 sp, ch 2, sk last ch-2 sp, sc in next 2 sts, ch 1, sc in last st; join with sl st in first sc – Seventy-two 2-sc groups, 36 ch-2 sps, and 36 ch-1 sps.

Rnd 26: With I, ch 3 (counts as dc), turn, dc in first st, ch 1, sk next ch-1 sp, dc in next 2 sts, *ch 2, sk next ch-2 sp, dc in next 2 sts, ch 1, sk next ch-1 sp, dc in next 2 sts; rep from * to last ch-2 sp, ch 2, sk last ch-2 sp; join with sl st in top of beg ch – Seventy-two 2-dc groups, 36 ch-2 sps, and 36 ch-1 sps.

Rnd 27: With I, ch 1, turn, sc in same ch as joining sl st, ch 2, sk next ch-2 sp, sc in next 2 sts, *ch 1, sk next ch-1 sp, sc in next 2 sts, ch 2, sk next ch-2 sp, sc in next 2 sts; rep from * to last ch-1 sp, ch 1, sk next ch-1 sp, sc in last st; join with sl st in first sc – Seventy-two 2-sc groups, 36 ch-2 sps, and 36 ch-1 sps.

Rnd 28: With I, ch 3 (counts as dc), turn, dc in first st, ch 2, sk next ch-1 sp, dc in next 2 sts, *ch 2, sk next ch-2 sp, dc in next 2 sts, ch 2, sk next ch-1 sp, dc in next 2 sts; rep from * to last ch-2 sp, ch 2, sk last ch-2 sp; join with sl st in top of beg ch – Seventy-two 2-dc groups and 72 ch-2 sps.
Fasten off.

Rnd 29: From WS, join H with sc in any st, work sc in each st and 2 sc in each ch-2 sp around; join with sl st in first sc – 288 sc.
Fasten off.

Triangle Points

Place a marker in any st of Rnd 29, *sk the next 23 sts, place a marker in the next st; rep from * until a total of 12 markers have been placed, with 23 sts between each of the marked sts.

First Triangle

Row 1 (RS): From RS, join J with sl st in 4th sc before any one of the marked sts, sk next 3 sts, (tr, 4 dc, ch 5, 4 dc, tr) in marked st, sk next 3 sts, sl st in next st – 2 tr, 8 dc, 2 sl sts, and 1 ch-5 sp.

Row 2: Ch 4 (counts as tr), do not turn, sk next 3 sts of last rnd of Afghan, sl st in next st, TURN, 2 dc in first tr of Row 1, dc in next 4 sts, (2 dc, ch 5, 2 dc) in ch-5 sp, dc in next 4 sts, (2 dc, tr) in last tr, sk next 3 sts of last rnd of Afghan, sl st in next st.
Fasten off.

Second through Twelfth Triangles

Work as for First Triangle.
Note that you will have 7 unworked sts of Rnd 29 between each of the Triangles. Remove markers.

Edging Rnd: From RS, join J with sl st in first st following ch-5 sp of any triangle point, ch 1, beg in same st as joining, *sc in next 9 sts (working last sc in top of beg ch-4), 3 dc in sl st, dc in next 3 sts of last rnd of Afghan, 2 dc in next st, dc in next 3 sts, 3 dc in first sl st of next triangle point, sc in next 9 sts to ch-5 sp, 5 sc in ch-5 sp; rep from * around; join with sl st in first sc – 444 sts.
Fasten off.

OUTER FLOWERS (make 12)

Color Sequence 1 (make 1): Work 1 rnd each with A, B, C, D, E, B.
Color Sequence 2 (make 1): Work 1 rnd each with A, C, D, E, B, C.
Color Sequence 3 (make 1): Work 1 rnd each with A, D, E, B, C, D.
Color Sequence 4 (make 1): Work 1 rnd each with A, E, B, C, D, E.
Color Sequence 5 (make 2): Work 1 rnd each with A, D, E, C, B, D.
Color Sequence 6 (make 2): Work 1 rnd each with A, E, C, B, D, E.
Color Sequence 7 (make 2): Work 1 rnd each with A, C, B, D, E, C.
Color Sequence 8 (make 2): Work 1 rnd each with A, B, D, E, C, B.

With A, ch 6; join with sl st in first ch to form a ring.

Rnds 1-6: Work same as Rnds 1-6 of Center Flower, changing color each rnd following color sequence – twenty-four 3-dc groups when Rnd 6 is completed.
Fasten off.

Rnds 7 and 8: With A, work same as Rnds 7 and 8 of Center Flower – Thirty-six 2-sc groups and 36 ch-1 sps in Rnd 8.
Fasten off.

Rnd 9: From RS, draw up a loop of F in first st of any 2-sc group, ch 2 (counts as hdc), hdc in next st, *ch 1, sk next ch-1 sp, hdc in next 2 sts; rep from * to last ch-1 sp, ch 1, sk last ch-1 sp; join with sl st in first sc – Thirty-six 2-hdc groups and 36 ch-1 sps.
Fasten off.

Rnd 10: From RS, join G with sc in any st, sc in each st and ch-1 sp around – 108 sc.
Fasten off.

Join Outer Flowers to Afghan
Use B, C, D, or E as desired, to join each Flower to Afghan.

Join First Flower: From RS of Afghan, join yarn with sl st in center sc of 5-sc group worked in ch-5 sp at tip of any triangle point on Afghan, ch 4, from RS, sl st in any st of Outer Flower, ch 4, sl st in same st of Afghan, ch 2, sk next 3 sts of Outer Flower, sl st in next st, ch 2, sk next st of Afghan, sl st in next st, *ch 2, sk next 2 sts of Outer Flower, sl st in next st, ch 2, sk next 2 sts of Afghan, sl st in next st; rep from * 10 more times, ch 2, sk next 2 sts of Outer Flower, sl st in next st, ch 2, sk next st of Afghan, sl st in next st (center st of 5-sc group), ch 4, sk next 3 sts of Outer Flower, sl st in next st, ch 4, sl st in same st of Afghan.
Fasten off.

Join Next Flower: From RS, join another color yarn with sl st in last st worked into on Afghan (at tip of triangle point), ch 4, insert hook in last st worked into on previous Outer Flower AND any st of next Outer Flower, yarn over and draw through all loops on hook (joining the 2 Flowers together with sl st), ch 4, sl st in same st of Afghan (at tip of triangle point), ch 2, sk next 3 sts of Outer Flower, sl st in next st, ch 2, sk next st of Afghan, sl st in next st, *ch 2, sk next 2 sts of Outer Flower, sl st in next st, ch 2, sk next 2 sts of Afghan, sl st in next st; rep from * 10 more times, ch 2, sk next 2 sts of Outer Flower, sl st in next st, ch 2, sk next st of Afghan, sl st in next st (center st of 5-sc group), ch 4, sk next 3 sts of Outer Flower, sl st in next st, ch 4, sl st in same st of Afghan.
Fasten off.

Rep until all Outer Flowers have been joined to Afghan. When working last sl st into last Outer Flower, insert hook into st of last Outer Flower AND into first st worked into on first Outer Flower.

FINISHING

Border

Border is worked from left to right (right to left if you are left-handed) – in other words, you're working in the opposite direction from which sts are usually worked.

Rnd 1 (RS): From RS of any Outer Flower, sk 4 unworked sts from the last sl st worked into Outer Flower when Flower was joined to Afghan, join J with sl st in next st, *(ch 3, sk next 2 sts, sl st in next st) 19 times, ch 2, sk last 4 unworked sts of current Outer Flower, sk next 4 unworked sts of next Outer Flower, sl st in next st; rep from * around working last sl st in first sl st.
Fasten off.

Weave in ends.

Outer Flower

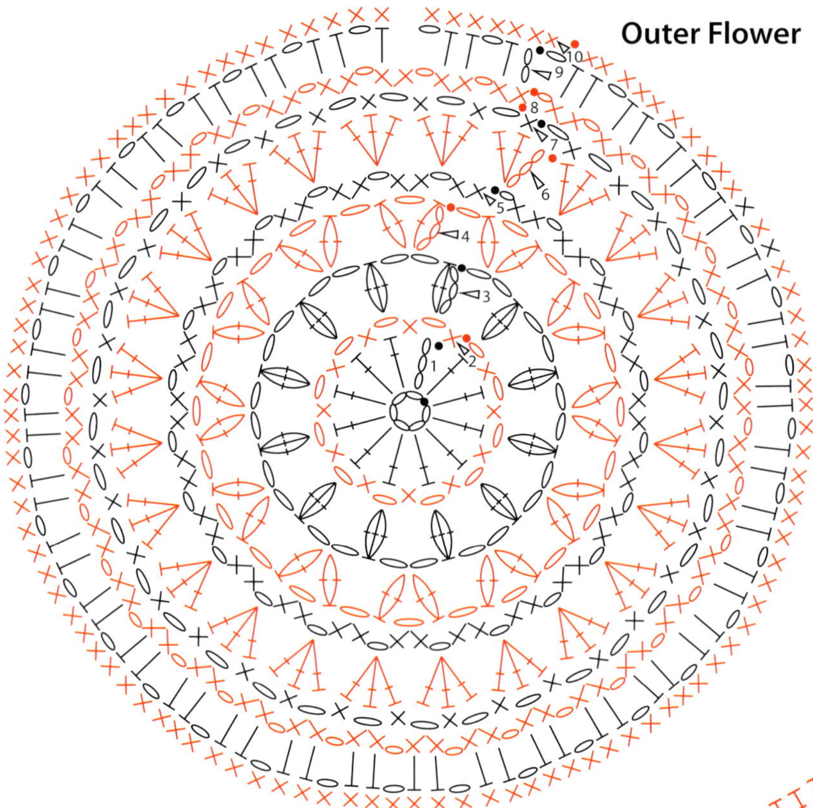

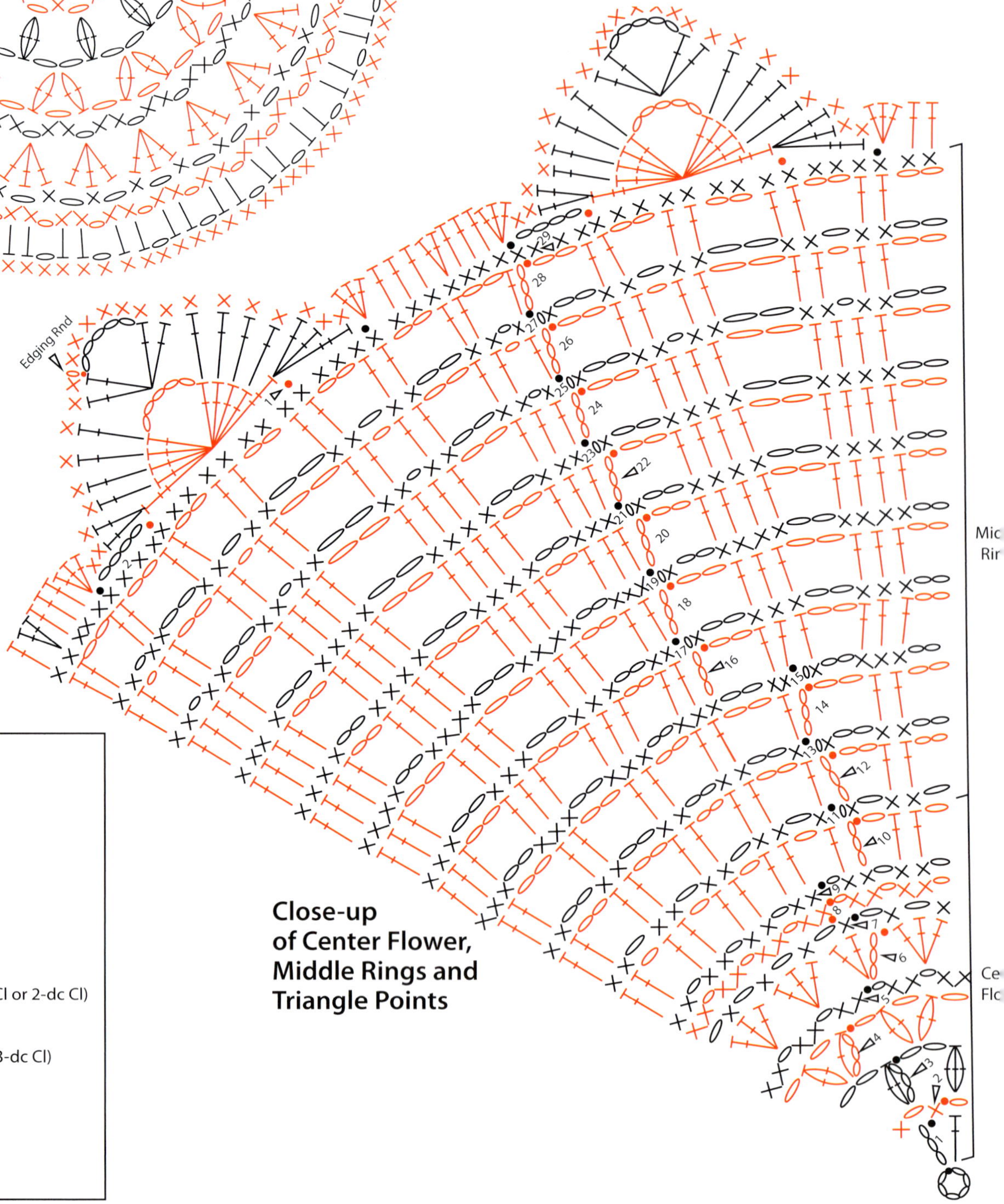

Close-up of Center Flower, Middle Rings and Triangle Points

KEY

- • = slip stitch (sl st)
- ⬭ = chain (ch)
- × = single crochet (sc)
- = half double crochet (hdc)
- = double crochet (dc)
- = 2-double crochet cluster (Cl or 2-dc Cl)
- = 3-double crochet cluster (3-dc Cl)
- = treble crochet (tr)
- ◁ = beg new color

Center Flower, Middle Rings and Triangle Points

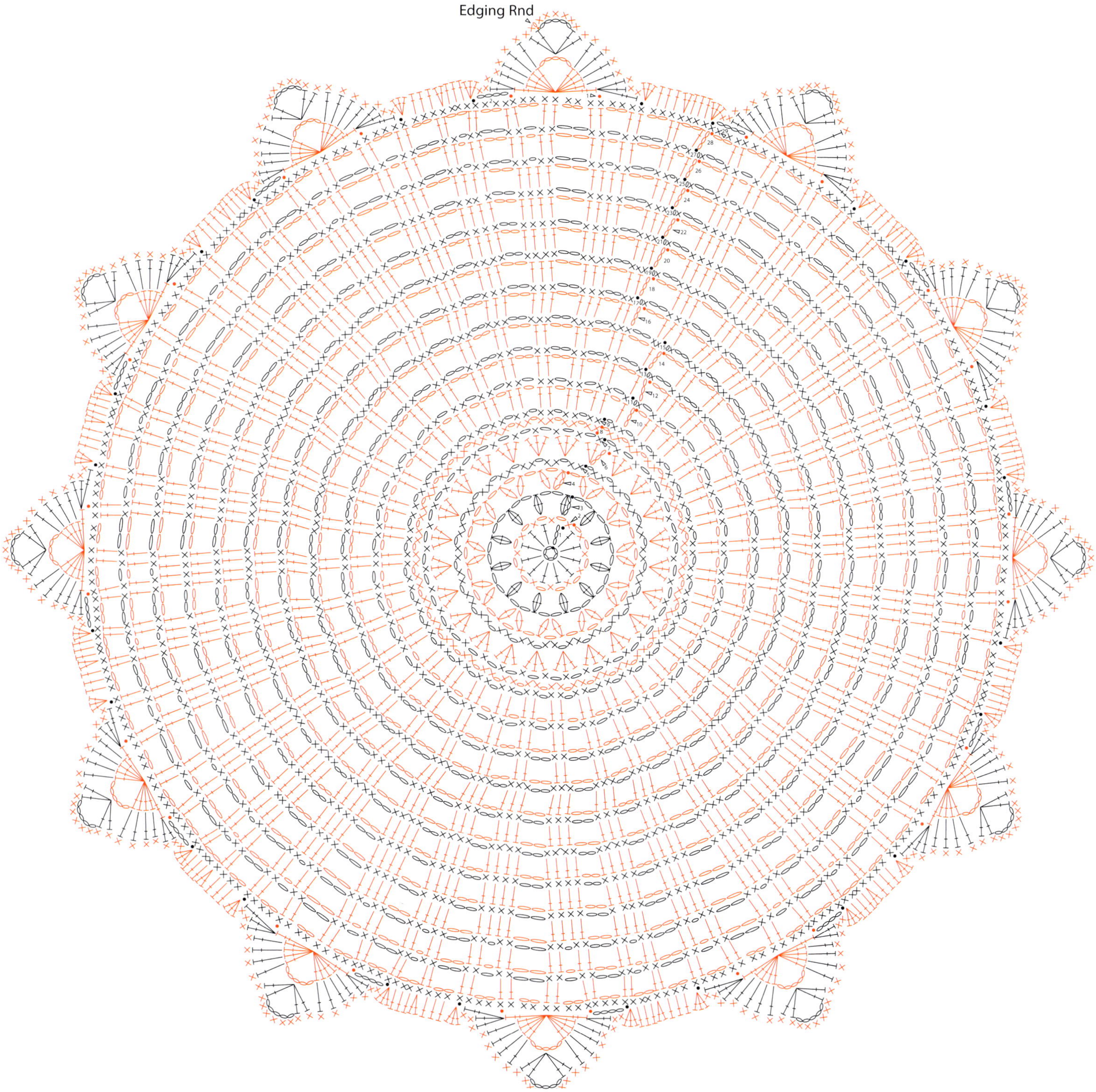

Framhurst Afghan

EASY +

SIZE

About 39" x 50" (99 cm x 127 cm)

Shopping List

Yarn (Medium Weight) MEDIUM 4

LION BRAND® VANNA'S CHOICE®

(Art. #860)

- ☐ #176 Peacock - 4 balls (A)
- ☐ #108 Dusty Blue - 3 balls (B)
- ☐ #105 Silver Blue - 1 ball (C)
- ☐ #106 Aquamarine - 1 ball (D)
- ☐ #099 Linen - 1 ball (E)

or colors of your choice

Crochet Hook

LION BRAND® crochet hook

- ☐ Size J-10 (6 mm)

or size needed for gauge

Additional Supply

- ☐ LION BRAND® large-eyed blunt needle

GAUGE

Square 1 = about 5½" x 5½" (14 cm x 14 cm).

BE SURE TO CHECK YOUR GAUGE.

NOTES

1. 24 Squares are made separately, then sewn together following a diagram.
2. Squares are worked in rnds, with RS always facing.
3. To change color, work last stitch of old color to last yarn over. Yarn over with new color and draw through all loops on hook to complete the stitch.

SQUARE 1 (Make 16 total: 6 using C for Rnds 1 and 2, 7 using D for Rnds 1 and 2, and 3 using E for Rnds 1 and 2)

With C (or yarn color as specified above), ch 4; join with sl st in first ch to make a ring.

Rnd 1: Ch 3 (counts as first dc here and throughout this pattern), 11 dc in ring; join with sl st in top of beg ch – 12 sts.

Rnd 2: Ch 3, dc in same st, 2 dc in each dc around; join with sl st in top of beg ch; change to B in last st – 24 sts.

Rnd 3: With B, ch 1, sc in same st, sc in next st, hdc in next st, 3 dc in next st, hdc in next st, sc in next st, *sc in next 2 sts, hdc in next st, 3 dc in next st, hdc in next st, sc in next st; rep from * twice more; join with sl st in first sc – 32 sts.

Rnd 4: Ch 3, dc in next 3 sts, 5 dc in next st, dc in next 3 sts, *dc in next 4 sts, 5 dc in next st, dc in next 3 sts; rep from * twice more; join with sl st in top of beg ch; change to A in last st – 48 sts.

Rnd 5: With A, ch 3, dc in next 5 sts, 5 dc in next st, dc in next 5 sts, *dc in next 6 sts, 5 dc in next st, dc in next 5 sts; rep from * twice more; join with sl st in top of beg ch – 64 sts. Fasten off.

SQUARE 2 (Make 5 total: 2 using C for Rnds 1-4, 2 using D for Rnds 1-4 and 1 using E for Rnds 1-4)

Rnds 1 and 2: Work as for Square 1, using yarn color as specified for Square 2.
At the end of Rnd 2, do not change to B, but continue with same yarn color.

Rnd 3: Ch 3, 2 dc in next st, *dc in next st, 2 dc in next st; rep from * around; join with sl st in top of beg ch – 36 sts.

Rnd 4: Ch 3, dc in next st, 2 dc in next st, *dc in next 2 sts, 2 dc in next st; rep from * around; join with sl st in top of beg ch; change to B in last st – 48 sts.

Rnd 5: With B, ch 1, sc in same st, sc in next 2 sts, hdc in next 2 sts, dc in next st, 5 dc in next st, dc in next st, hdc in next 2 sts, sc in next 2 sts, *sc in next 3 sts, hdc in next 2 sts, dc in next st, 5 dc in next st, dc in next st, hdc in next 2 sts, sc in next 2 sts; rep from * twice more; join with sl st in first sc – 64 sts.

Rnd 6: Ch 3, dc in next 7 sts, 5 dc in next st, dc in next 7 sts, *dc in next 8 sts, 5 dc in next st, dc in next 7 sts; rep from * twice more; join with sl st in top of beg ch – 80 sts.

Rnd 7: Ch 3, dc in each dc, working 5 dc in each corner; join with sl st in top of beg ch; change to A in last st – 96 sts.

Rnds 8 and 9: With A, ch 3, dc in each dc, working 5 dc in each corner; join with sl st in top of beg ch – 128 sts at the end of Rnd 9.
Fasten off.

SQUARE 3 (Make 3: 1 each using C, D, and E for Rnds 1-6)

Rnds 1-3: Work as for Square 2, using yarn color as specified for Square 3.

Rnd 4: Ch 3, dc in next st, 2 dc in next st, *dc in next 2 sts, 2 dc in next st; rep from * around; join with sl st in top of beg ch – 48 sts.

Rnd 5: Ch 3, dc in next 2 sts, 2 dc in next st, *dc in next 3 sts, 2 dc in next st; rep from * around; join with sl st in top of beg ch – 60 sts.

Rnd 6: Ch 3, dc in next 3 sts, 2 dc in next st, *dc in next 4 sts, 2 dc in next st; rep from * around; join with sl st in top of beg ch; change to B in last st – 72 sts.

Rnd 7: With B, ch 1, sc in same st, sc in next 3 sts, hdc in next 3 sts, dc in next 2 sts, 3 tr in next st, dc in next 2 sts, hdc in next 3 sts, sc in next 3 sts, *sc in next 4 sts, hdc in next 3 sts, dc in next 2 sts, 3 tr in next st, dc in next 2 sts, hdc in next 3 sts, sc in next 3 sts; rep from * twice more; join with sl st in first sc – 80 sts.

Rnd 8: Ch 1, sc in same st, sc in next 3 sts, hdc in next 3 sts, dc in next 2 sts, tr in next st, 5 tr in next st, tr in next st, dc in next 2 sts, hdc in next 3 sts, sc in next 3 sts, *sc in next 4 sts, hdc in next 3 sts, dc in next 2 sts, tr in next st, 5 tr in next st, tr in next st, dc in next 2 sts, hdc in next 3 sts, sc in next 3 sts; rep from * twice more; join with sl st in first sc – 96 sts.

Rnd 9: Ch 3, dc in next 11 sts, 5 dc in next st, dc in next 11 sts, *dc in next 12 sts, 5 dc in next st, dc in next 11 sts; rep from * twice more; join with sl st in top of beg ch – 112 sts.

Rnds 10 and 11: Ch 3, dc in each dc, working 5 dc in each corner; join with sl st in top of beg ch; change to A in last st of Rnd 11 – 144 sts at the end of Rnd 11.

Rnds 12–14: With A, ch 3, dc in each dc, working 5 dc in each corner; join with sl st in top of beg ch – 192 sts at the end of Rnd 14.
Fasten off.

FINISHING

Following diagram, sew Squares together.

Edging

From RS, join A with sl st anywhere along outside edge of Afghan; ch 3, work dc evenly spaced around outside edge of Afghan, working 5 dc in each corner; join with sl st in top of beg ch.
Fasten off.

Weave in ends.

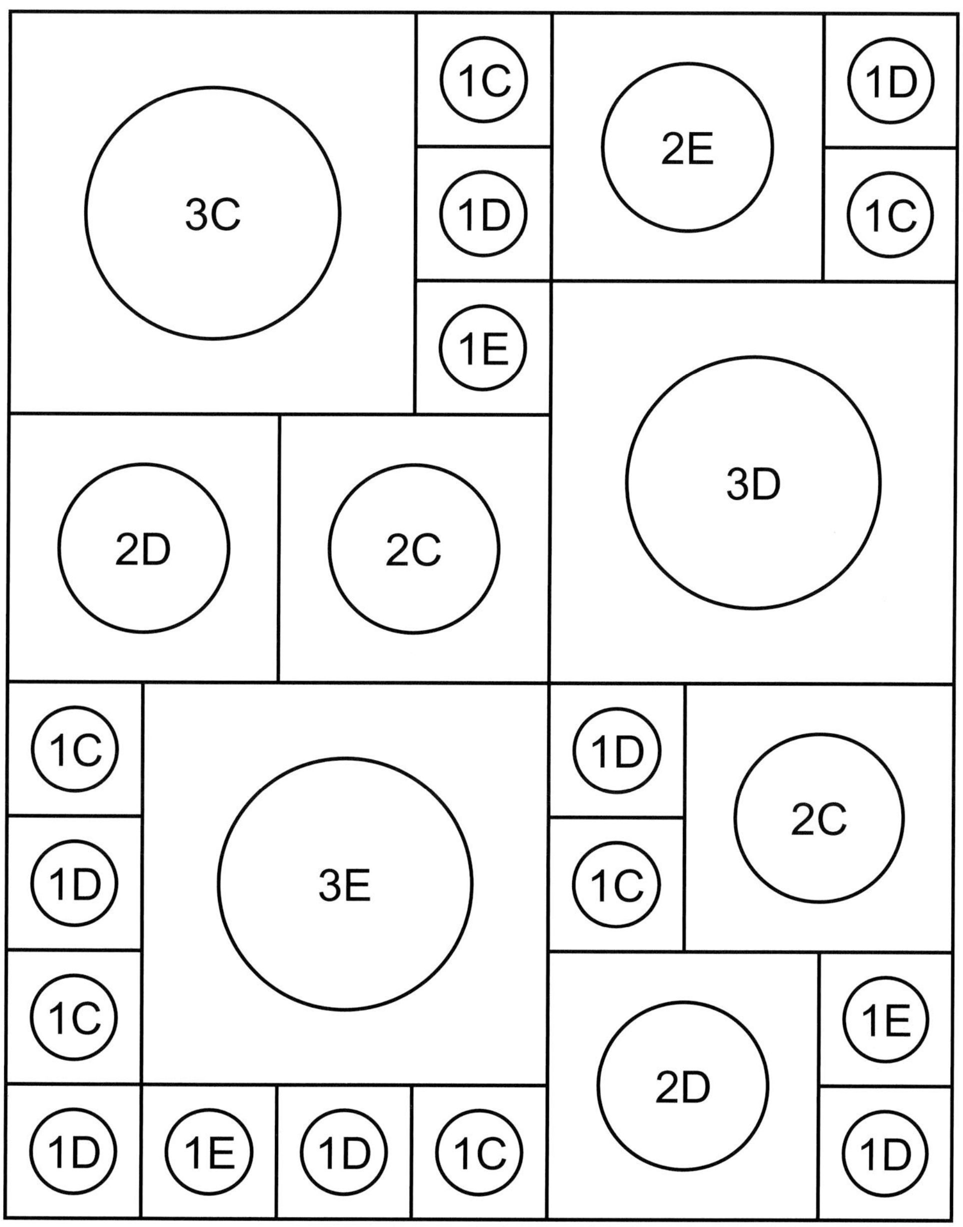

KEY
C = #105 Silver Blue
D = #106 Aquamarine
E = #099 Linen

Newport Baby Afghan

EASY +

SIZE

About 32" x 38" (81.5 cm x 96.5 cm)

Shopping List

Yarn (Medium Weight) MEDIUM 4

LION BRAND® VANNA'S CHOICE®
(Art. #860)

- ☐ #100 White - 4 balls (A)
- ☐ #158 Mustard - 1 ball (B)
- ☐ #104 Pink Grapefruit - 1 ball (C)
- ☐ #139 Rose Shocking - 1 ball (D)
- ☐ #102 Aqua - 1 ball (E)
- ☐ #106 Aquamarine - 1 ball (F)
- ☐ #111 Sky Blue - 1 ball (G)
- ☐ #183 Periwinkle - 1 ball (H)

or colors of your choice

Crochet Hook

LION BRAND® crochet hook

- ☐ Size I-9 (5.5 mm)

or size needed for gauge

Additional Supply

- ☐ LION BRAND® large-eyed blunt needle

GAUGE

1 Hexagon = about 5" (12.5 cm) measured diagonally from one corner to opposite corner.

BE SURE TO CHECK YOUR GAUGE.

STITCH GUIDE

TREBLE CROCHET DECREASE WORKED OVER 3 STITCHES (abbreviated tr2tog-over-3)

(Yarn over) twice, insert hook in next tr and draw up a loop, (yarn over and draw through 2 loops) twice, skip next sc of Rnd 3, (yarn over) twice, insert hook in first ch of ch-5 foundation ch of next point and draw up a loop, (yarn over and draw through 2 loops) twice, yarn over and draw through all 3 loops on hook.

NOTES

1. 59 Hexagons are worked, then sewn together following a diagram to make the Afghan.
2. Each Hexagon is worked in joined rnds with RS always facing. A star-shaped center is worked first. Sts are worked around star to shape piece into a hexagon.
3. A stitch diagram is provided to clarify the Hexagons.

HEXAGON (make 59)

Make 8 using B for center star, 7 using C for center star, 11 using D for center star, 8 using E for center star, 9 using F for center star, 7 using G for center star, and 9 using H for center star.

Center Star

Ch 4; join with sl st in first ch to form a ring.

Rnd 1 (RS): Ch 2 (counts as hdc), work 11 more hdc in ring; join with sl st in top of beg ch –12 hdc.

Rnd 2: Ch 1, 2 sc in same st as joining and in each st around; join with sl st in first sc – 24 sc.

Rnd 3: Ch 1, sc in same st as joining, *ch 5, working in back bumps of ch, sc in 2nd ch from hook, hdc in next ch, dc in next ch, tr in next ch (point made), sk next 3 sts of Rnd 2, sc in next st; rep from * around omitting last sc; join with sl st in first sc – 6 points and 6 sc.

Fasten off.

Shape into Hexagon

Rnd 4 (RS): From RS, working in back loops only, draw up a loop of A in any hdc, ch 2 (counts as hdc), *dc in next dc, tr2tog-over-3; continuing across foundation ch of point, dc in next ch, hdc in next ch, sc in next ch, sl st in skipped ch at tip of point; working in sts along other side of point, sc in next sc, hdc in next hdc; rep from * around omitting last hdc; join with sl st in top of beg ch – 48 sts (including the sl sts).

Rnd 5: Ch 1, *sc in each st to next sl st at tip of point, 2 sc in sl st; rep from * 5 more times, sc in last st; join with sl st in first sc – 54 sc (9 sc on each of 6 sides).

Fasten off.

FINISHING

Following diagram, sew Hexagons into 9 strips with color of center stars in the following orders:

Strip #1: F, B, D, H, E, D, H.

Strip #2: C, F, H, D, G, E.

Strip #3: E, H, D, B, F, C, B.

Strip #4: C, E, G, C, E, G.

Strip #5: B, H, C, F, B, D, F.

Strip #6: D, G, H, D, H, E.

Strip #7: E, F, D, B, F, D, H.

Strip #8: C, G, E, C, B, F.

Strip #9: G, B, D, F, H, D, G.

Sew strips together to make Afghan.

Weave in ends.

KEY

- #100 White (A)
- #158 Mustard (B)
- #104 Pink Grapefruit (C)
- #139 Rose Shocking (D)
- #102 Aqua (E)
- #106 Aquamarine (F)
- #111 Sky Blue (G)
- #183 Periwinkle (H)

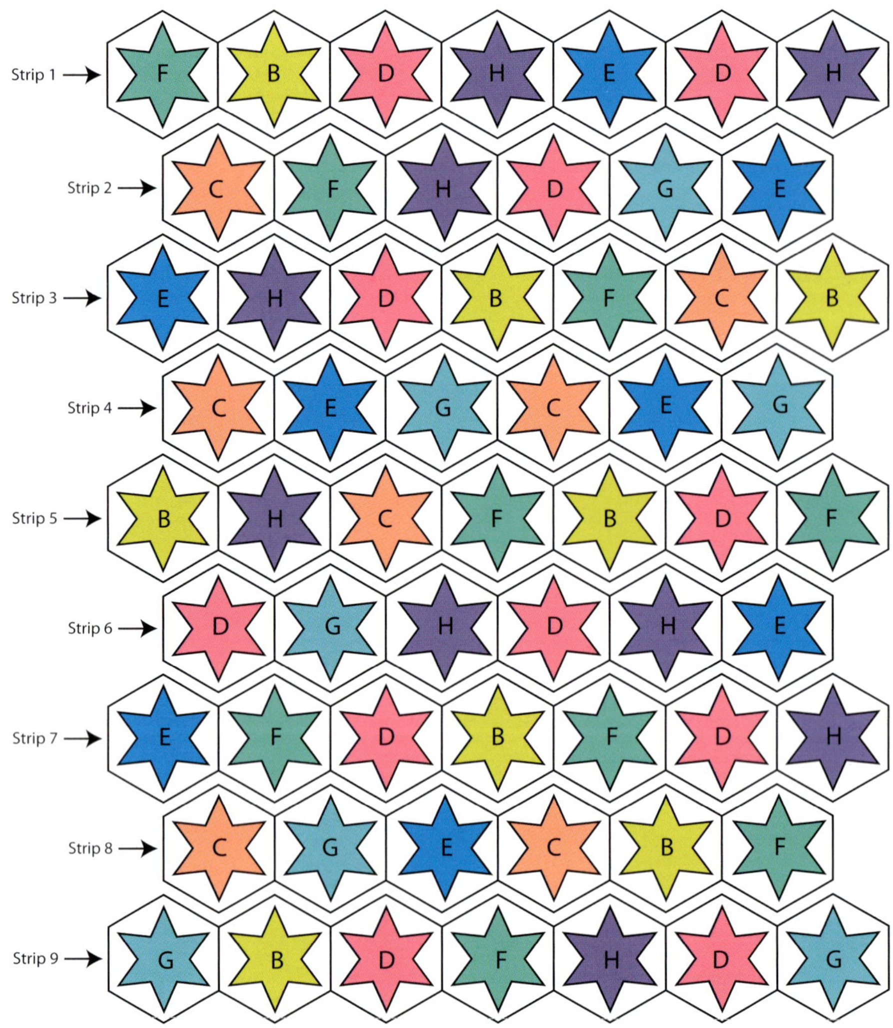

Hexagon

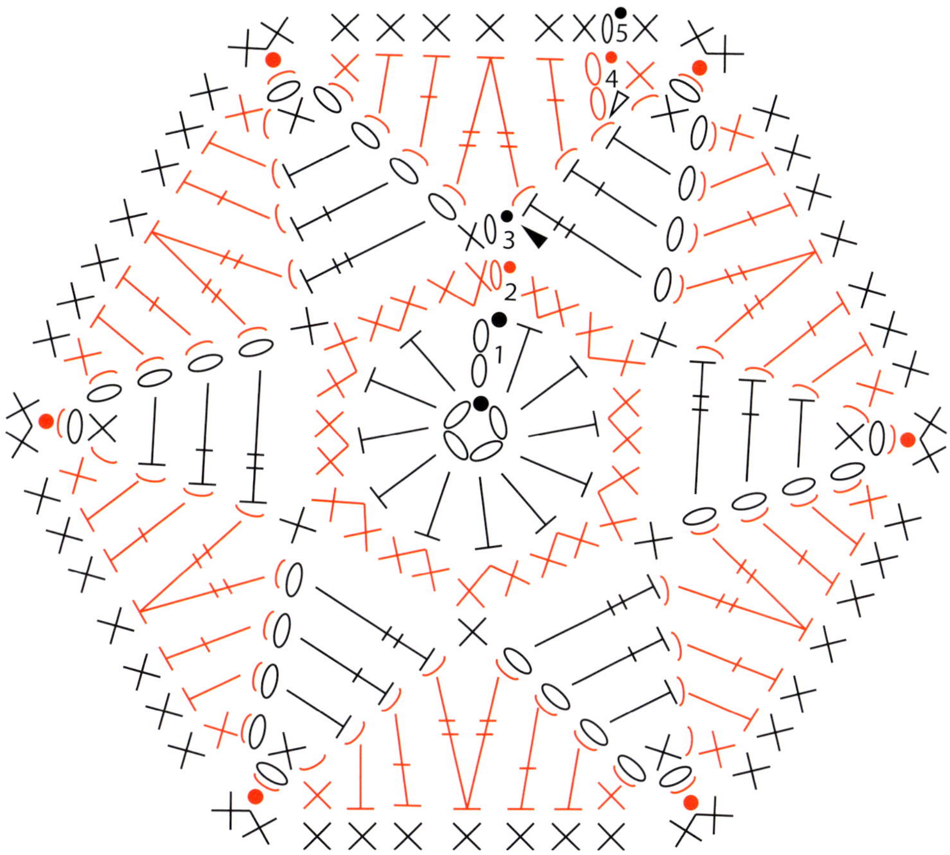

KEY

- ● = slip stitch (sl st)
- = chain (ch)
- = single crochet (sc)
- = half double crochet (hdc)
- = double crochet (dc)
- = treble crochet (tr)
- = treble crochet 2 together worked over 3 stitches (tr2tog-over-3)
- = work in back loop only
- = draw up a loop
- = fasten off

Ozark Star Mandala Afghan

EASY +

SIZE

About 56" (142 cm) wide, from corner to corner

Shopping List

Yarn (Medium Weight) MEDIUM 4

LION BRAND® VANNA'S CHOICE® (Art. #860)

- ☐ #148 Burgundy - 2 balls (A)
- ☐ #173 Dusty Green - 1 ball (B)
- ☐ #130 Honey - 2 balls (C)
- ☐ #108 Dusty Blue - 1 ball (D)
- ☐ #176 Peacock - 1 ball (E)
- ☐ #123 Beige - 3 balls (F)

or colors of your choice

Crochet Hook

LION BRAND® crochet hook

- ☐ Size I-9 (5.5 mm)

or size needed for gauge

Additional Supply

- ☐ LION BRAND® large-eyed blunt needle

GAUGE

1 Diamond = about 4½" x 6½" (11.5 cm x 16.5 cm).

BE SURE TO CHECK YOUR GAUGE.

NOTES

1. 108 Diamonds are worked, then sewn together following a diagram.
2. Each Diamond is worked in joined rnds with RS always facing. Do not turn at beginning of rnds.
3. A Border is worked around outside edge of assembled Afghan.
4. For those who find a visual helpful, we've included stitch diagrams.

DIAMOND (make 108)

Make 18 with A, 12 with B, 24 with C, 12 with D, 12 with E, and 30 with F.

Ch 6; join with sl st in first ch to form a ring.

Rnd 1 (RS): Ch 6 (counts a dc, ch 3), (dc, hdc, 3 sc, hdc, dc, ch 3, dc, hdc, 3 sc, hdc) in ring; join with sl st in 3rd ch of beg ch – 14 sts and 2 ch-3 sps .

Rnd 2: Sl st in first ch-3 sp, ch 6 (counts as dc, ch 3), 3 dc in same ch-3 sp, dc in next 3 sts, (dc, ch 2, dc) in next st, dc in next 3 sts, (3 dc, ch 3, 3 dc) in next ch-3 sp, dc in next 3 sts, (dc, ch 2, dc) in next st, dc in next 3 sts, 2 dc in first ch-3 sp; join with sl st in 3rd ch of beg ch – 28 sts, 2 ch-3 sps, and 2 ch-2 sps (7 sts across each of 4 sides between ch-sps).

Rnd 3: Sl st in first ch-3 sp, ch 7 (counts as dc, ch 4), 3 dc in same ch-3 sp, ch 1, sk next st, dc in next 3 sts, ch 1, sk next st, dc in next 2 sts, (dc, ch 2, dc) in next ch-2 sp, dc in next 2 sts, ch 1, sk next st, dc in next 3 sts, ch 1, sk next st, (3 dc, ch 4, 3 dc) in next ch-3 sp, ch 1, sk next st, dc in next 3 sts, ch 1, sk next st, dc in next 2 sts, (dc, ch 2, dc) in next ch-2 sp, dc in next 2 sts, ch 1, sk next st, dc in next 3 sts, ch 1, sk next st, 2 dc in first ch-3 sp; join with sl st in 3rd ch of beg ch – 36 sts, 2 ch-4 sps, 2 ch-2 sps, and 8 ch-1 sps (Twelve 3-dc groups; one 3-dc group between ch-sps). Fasten off.

FINISHING

Sew Diamonds together following diagram.

Border

From RS, join F with sl st in ch-2 sp of D-colored Diamond at any corner.

Rnd 1: Ch 1, beg in same ch-2 sp, *(sc, hdc, sc) in ch-2 sp; work 1 sc in each dc and ch-sp across edges of Diamonds to ch-4 sp of F-colored Diamond about halfway between corners, dc in F-colored ch-4 sp, tr in ch-4 sp at tip of D-colored Diamond between F-colored Diamonds, dc in ch-4 sp of next F-colored Diamond; sc in each dc and ch-sp across edges of Diamonds to ch-2 sp of D-colored Diamond at next corner; rep from * all the way around outer edge; join with sl st in first sc.

Rnd 2: Ch 3 (counts as dc), turn, dc in each st around working (dc, tr, dc) in hdc at each corner; join with sl st in top of beg ch.
Fasten off.

Rnd 3: From RS, draw up a loop of A in any st, ch 3 (counts as dc), dc in each st around working (dc, tr, dc) in tr at each corner; join with sl st in top of beg ch.

Rnd 4: Ch 1, turn, sc in each st around working (sc, hdc, sc) in tr at each corner; join with sl st in first sc.
Fasten off.

Weave in ends.

KEY

- ● = slip stitch (sl st)
- ⬭ = chain (ch)
- × = single crochet (sc)
- = half double crochet (hdc)
- = double crochet (dc)
- = treble crochet (tr)

Diamond

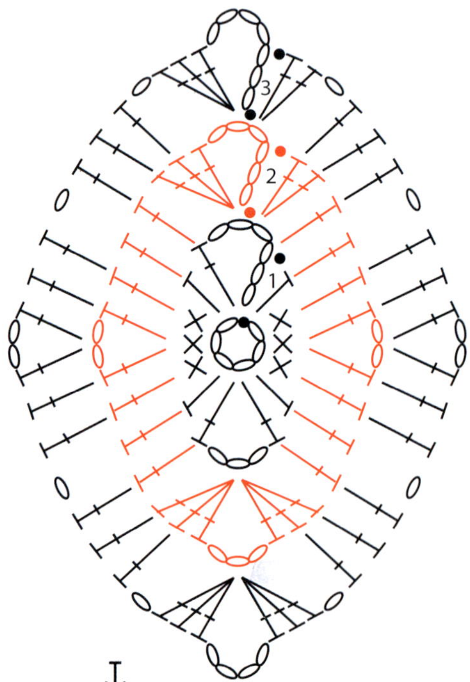

Border
(reduced sample)

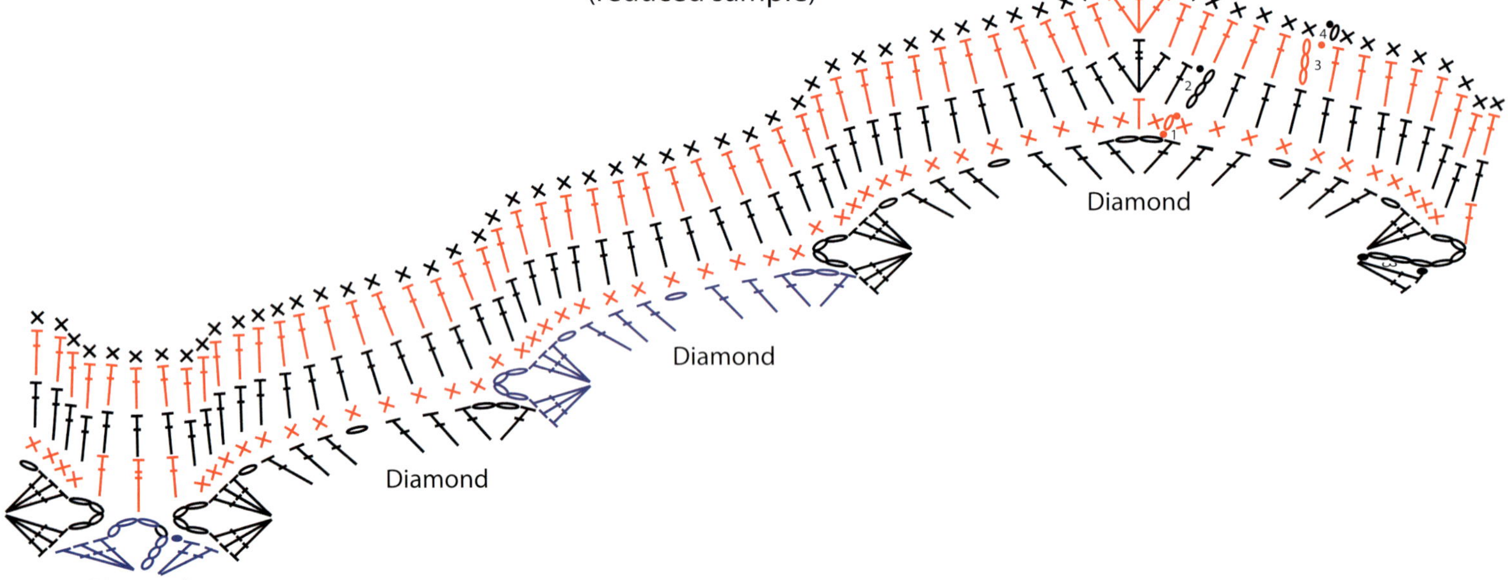

KEY

- = #148 Burgundy (A)
- = #173 Dusty Green (B)
- = #130 Honey (C)
- = #108 Dusty Blue (D)
- = #176 Peacock (E)
- = #123 Beige (F)

Rainbow Mandala Afghan

EASY +

SIZE

About 45" (114.5 cm) diameter

Shopping List

Yarn (Medium Weight) MEDIUM 4

LION BRAND® VANNA'S CHOICE®

(Art. #860)

- ☐ #098 Fisherman - 2 balls (A)
- ☐ #139 Rose Shocking - 1 ball (B)
- ☐ #113 Scarlet - 1 ball (C)
- ☐ #134 Terracotta - 1 ball (D)
- ☐ #158 Mustard - 1 ball (E)
- ☐ #172 Kelly Green - 1 ball (F)
- ☐ #174 Olive - 1 ball (G)
- ☐ #176 Peacock - 1 ball (H)
- ☐ #109 Colonial Blue - 1 ball (I)
- ☐ #147 Purple - 1 ball (J)
- ☐ #145 Eggplant - 1 ball (K)

  or colors of your choice

Crochet Hook

LION BRAND® crochet hook

- ☐ Size J-10 (6 mm)

  or size needed for gauge

Additional Supply

- ☐ LION BRAND® large-eyed blunt needle

GAUGE

6½ rnds = about 4" (10 cm) in dc.

BE SURE TO CHECK YOUR GAUGE.

NOTES

1. Afghan is worked in one piece in joined rnds with RS always facing.
2. The yarn color is changed on every 3rd rnd.
3. Change yarn color by fastening off old color and joining the new color. Join the new color in a different st than last st worked so that increases do not line up.

AFGHAN

With A, ch 4; join with sl st in first ch to form a ring.

Rnd 1 (RS): Ch 4 (counts as dc, ch 1), dc in ring, (ch 1, dc in ring) 6 times, ch 1; join with sl st in 3rd ch of beg ch – 8 dc and 8 ch-1 sps.

Rnd 2: Ch 3 (counts as dc), dc in same st as joining, dc in next ch-1 sp, (2 dc in next dc, dc in next ch-1 sp; rep from * around; join with sl st in top of beg ch – 24 dc.

Rnd 3: Ch 3 (counts as dc), 2 dc in next st, *dc in next st, 2 dc in next st; rep from * around; join with sl st in top of beg ch – 36 dc.

Fasten off.

Rnd 4: From RS, draw up a loop of B in any st, ch 3 (counts as dc), dc in next st, 2 dc in next st, *dc in next 2 sts, 2 dc in next st; rep from * around; join with sl st in top of beg ch – 48 dc.

Rnd 5: Ch 3 (counts as dc), dc in next 2 sts, 2 dc in next st, *dc in next 3 sts, 2 dc in next st; rep from * around; join with sl st in top of beg ch – 60 dc.

Rnd 6: Ch 3 (counts as dc), dc in next 3 sts, 2 dc in next st, *dc in next 4 sts, 2 dc in next st; rep from * around; join with sl st in top of beg ch – 72 dc.

Fasten off.

Rnd 7: From RS, draw up a loop of C in any st, ch 3 (counts as dc), dc in next 4 sts, 2 dc in next st, *dc in next 5 sts, 2 dc in next st; rep from * around; join with sl st in top of beg ch – 84 dc.

Rnd 8: Ch 3 (counts as dc), dc in next 5 sts, 2 dc in next st, *dc in next 6 sts, 2 dc in next st; rep from * around; join with sl st in top of beg ch – 96 dc.

Rnd 9: Ch 3 (counts as dc), dc in next 6 sts, 2 dc in next st, *dc in next 7 sts, 2 dc in next st; rep from * around; join with sl st in top of beg ch – 108 dc.
Fasten off.

Rnd 10: From RS, draw up a loop of D in any st, ch 3 (counts as dc), dc in next 7 sts, 2 dc in next st, *dc in next 8 sts, 2 dc in next st; rep from * around; join with sl st in top of beg ch – 120 dc.

Rnd 11: Ch 3 (counts as dc), dc in next 8 sts, 2 dc in next st, *dc in next 9 sts, 2 dc in next st; rep from * around; join with sl st in top of beg ch – 132 dc.

Rnd 12: Ch 3 (counts as dc), dc in next 9 sts, 2 dc in next st, *dc in next 10 sts, 2 dc in next st; rep from * around; join with sl st in top of beg ch – 144 dc.
Fasten off.

Rnd 13: From RS, draw up a loop of E in any st, ch 3 (counts as dc), dc in next 10 sts, 2 dc in next st, *dc in next 11 sts, 2 dc in next st; rep from * around; join with sl st in top of beg ch – 156 dc.

Rnd 14: Ch 3 (counts as dc), dc in next 11 sts, 2 dc in next st, *dc in next 12 sts, 2 dc in next st; rep from * around; join with sl st in top of beg ch – 168 dc.

Rnd 15: Ch 3 (counts as dc), dc in next 12 sts, 2 dc in next st, *dc in next 13 sts, 2 dc in next st; rep from * around; join with sl st in top of beg ch – 180 dc.
Fasten off.

Rnd 16: From RS, draw up a loop of F in any st, ch 3 (counts as dc), dc in next 13 sts, 2 dc in next st, *dc in next 14 sts, 2 dc in next st; rep from * around; join with sl st in top of beg ch – 192 dc.

Rnd 17: Ch 3 (counts as dc), dc in next 14 sts, 2 dc in next st, *dc in next 15 sts, 2 dc in next st; rep from * around; join with sl st in top of beg ch – 204 dc.

Rnd 18: Ch 3 (counts as dc), dc in next 15 sts, 2 dc in next st, *dc in next 16 sts, 2 dc in next st; rep from * around; join with sl st in top of beg ch – 216 dc.
Fasten off.

Rnd 19: From RS, draw up a loop of G in any st, ch 3 (counts as dc), dc in next 16 sts, 2 dc in next st, *dc in next 17 sts, 2 dc in next st; rep from * around; join with sl st in top of beg ch – 228 dc.

Rnd 20: Ch 3 (counts as dc), dc in next 17 sts, 2 dc in next st, *dc in next 18 sts, 2 dc in next st; rep from * around; join with sl st in top of beg ch – 240 dc.

Rnd 21: Ch 3 (counts as dc), dc in next 18 sts, 2 dc in next st, *dc in next 19 sts, 2 dc in next st; rep from * around; join with sl st in top of beg ch – 252 dc.
Fasten off.

Rnd 22: From RS, draw up a loop of H in any st, ch 3 (counts as dc), dc in next 19 sts, 2 dc in next st, *dc in next 20 sts, 2 dc in next st; rep from * around; join with sl st in top of beg ch – 264 dc.

Rnd 23: Ch 3 (counts as dc), dc in next 20 sts, 2 dc in next st, *dc in next 21 sts, 2 dc in next st; rep from * around; join with sl st in top of beg ch – 276 dc.

Rnd 24: Ch 3 (counts as dc), dc in next 21 sts, 2 dc in next st, *dc in next 22 sts, 2 dc in next st; rep from * around; join with sl st in top of beg ch – 288 dc.
Fasten off.

Rnd 25: From RS, draw up a loop of I in any st, ch 3 (counts as dc), dc in next 22 sts, 2 dc in next st, *dc in next 23 sts, 2 dc in next st; rep from * around; join with sl st in top of beg ch – 300 dc.

Rnd 26: Ch 3 (counts as dc), dc in next 23 sts, 2 dc in next st, *dc in next 24 sts, 2 dc in next st; rep from * around; join with sl st in top of beg ch – 312 dc.

Rnd 27: Ch 3 (counts as dc), dc in next 24 sts, 2 dc in next st, *dc in next 25 sts, 2 dc in next st; rep from * around; join with sl st in top of beg ch – 324 dc.
Fasten off.

Rnd 28: From RS, draw up a loop of J in any st, ch 3 (counts as dc), dc in next 25 sts, 2 dc in next st, *dc in next 26 sts, 2 dc in next st; rep from * around; join with sl st in top of beg ch – 336 dc.

Rnd 29: Ch 3 (counts as dc), dc in next 26 sts, 2 dc in next st, *dc in next 27 sts, 2 dc in next st; rep from * around; join with sl st in top of beg ch – 348 dc.

Rnd 30: Ch 3 (counts as dc), dc in next 27 sts, 2 dc in next st, *dc in next 28 sts, 2 dc in next st; rep from * around; join with sl st in top of beg ch – 360 dc.
Fasten off.

Rnd 31: From RS, draw up a loop of K in any st, ch 3 (counts as dc), dc in next 28 sts, 2 dc in next st, *dc in next 29 sts, 2 dc in next st; rep from * around; join with sl st in top of beg ch – 372 dc.

Rnd 32: Ch 3 (counts as dc), dc in next 29 sts, 2 dc in next st, *dc in next 30 sts, 2 dc in next st; rep from * around; join with sl st in top of beg ch – 384 dc.

Rnd 33: Ch 3 (counts as dc), dc in next 30 sts, 2 dc in next st, *dc in next 31 sts, 2 dc in next st; rep from * around; join with sl st in top of beg ch – 396 dc.
Fasten off.

Rnd 34: From RS, draw up a loop of A in any st, ch 3 (counts as dc), dc in next 31 sts, 2 dc in next st, *dc in next 32 sts, 2 dc in next st; rep from * around; join with sl st in top of beg ch – 408 dc.

Rnd 35: Ch 3 (counts as dc), dc in next 32 sts, 2 dc in next st, *dc in next 33 sts, 2 dc in next st; rep from * around; join with sl st in top of beg ch – 420 dc.

Rnd 36: Ch 3 (counts as dc), dc in next 33 sts, 2 dc in next st, *dc in next 34 sts, 2 dc in next st; rep from * around; join with sl st in top of beg ch – 432 dc.

Edging Rnd: Sl st in each st around.
Fasten off.

FINISHING

Weave in ends.

Rockwell Mandala Afghan

EASY +

SIZE

About 45" x 60" (114.5 cm x 152.5 cm)

Shopping List

Yarn (Medium Weight) MEDIUM 4

LION BRAND® VANNA'S CHOICE®
(Art. #860)

- ☐ #100 White - 1 ball (A)
- ☐ #153 Black - 2 balls (B)
- ☐ #151 Charcoal Grey - 3 balls (C)
- ☐ #149 Silver Grey - 2 balls (D)
- ☐ #405 Silver Heather - 2 balls (E)
- ☐ #158 Mustard - 2 balls (F)

or colors of your choice

Crochet Hook

LION BRAND® crochet hook

- ☐ Size I-9 (5.5 mm)

or size needed for gauge

Additional Supply

- ☐ LION BRAND® large-eyed blunt needle

GAUGE

1 Small Square = about 5¼" x 5¼"
(13.5 cm x 13.5 cm).
BE SURE TO CHECK YOUR GAUGE.

TECHNIQUE EXPLANATION

Adjustable Ring Method

Wrap yarn around index finger. Insert hook into ring on finger, yarn over and draw up a loop. Carefully slip ring from finger and work the stitches of Rnd 1 (in pattern, below) into the ring. When Rnd 1 is complete, gently but firmly, pull yarn tail to tighten center of ring.

NOTES

1. 13 Large Squares and 14 smaller Mitered Squares are worked separately, then sewn together following a diagram.
2. Large Squares are worked in joined rnds with RS always facing.
3. Rnds 1 and 2 of Mitered Squares are worked same as the Large Squares, then Mitered Squares are worked back and forth in rows over only 2 sides of center square.
4. To change yarn color when working in **rnds**, fasten off old color and draw up a loop of new color in same st as joining.
5. To change yarn color when working in **rows**, work last st of old color to last yarn over. Yarn over with new color and draw through all loops on hook to complete st. Proceed with new color. Fasten off old color. Leave long tails to weave in later.

LARGE SQUARE I (make 5)

With A, make an adjustable ring.

Rnd 1 (RS): Ch 3 (counts as dc), work 11 more dc in ring; join with sl st in top of beg ch – 12 dc. Gently but firmly, pull yarn tail to tighten center of ring.

Rnd 2: Ch 1, beg in same st as joining, *(sc, hdc, sc) in next st (corner made), sc in next 2 sts; rep from * 3 more times; join with sl st in first sc – 4 sc along each of 4 sides plus 1 hdc at each corner.
Fasten off.

Rnd 3: From RS, draw up a loop of B in any corner hdc, ch 3 (counts as dc), (tr, dc) in same hdc, *dc in each st to next corner hdc, (dc, tr, dc) in corner hdc; rep from * 2 more times, dc in each st to end of rnd; join with sl st in top of beg ch – 6 dc along each of 4 sides plus 1 tr at each corner.

Rnd 4: (Sl st, sc, hdc, sc) in first corner tr, *sc in each st to next corner tr, (sc, hdc, sc) in corner tr; rep from * 2 more times, sc in each st to end of rnd; join with sl st in first sc – 8 sc along each of 4 sides plus 1 hdc at each corner.

Rnd 5: Ch 3 (counts as dc), (dc, tr, 2 dc) in corner hdc, *dc in each st to next corner hdc, (2 dc, tr, 2 dc) in corner hdc; rep from * 2 more times, dc in each st to end of rnd; join with sl st in top of beg ch – 12 dc along each of 4 sides plus 1 tr at each corner.
Fasten off.

Rnds 6-11: Rep Rnds 4 and 5 three more times, working Rnds 6-8 with C, Rnds 9-10 with D, and Rnd 11 with E – 30 dc along each of 4 sides plus 1 tr at each corner at the end of Rnd 11.
Do NOT fasten off.

Rnd 12: With E, rep Rnd 4 – 32 sc along each of 4 sides plus 1 hdc at each corner.
Fasten off.

LARGE SQUARE II
(make 4)

Make same as Large Square I, working Rnds 1 and 2 with A, Rnds 3 and 4 with F, Rnd 5 with E, Rnds 6 and 7 with D, Rnds 8-10 with C, and Rnds 11 and 12 with B.

LARGE SQUARE III
(make 4)

Make same as Large Square I, working Rnds 1 and 2 with A, Rnds 3 and 4 with B, Rnd 5 with C, Rnds 6-8 with D, Rnd 9 with E, and Rnds 10-12 with F.

MITERED SQUARE I
(make 4)

With A, make an adjustable ring.

Rnds 1 and 2 (RS): Rep Rnds 1 and 2 of Large Square.

Row 3: Draw up a loop of B in any corner hdc, ch 3 (counts as dc), dc in same hdc, dc in each st to next corner hdc, (dc, tr, dc) in corner hdc, dc in each st to next corner hdc, 2 dc in corner hdc; leave remaining sts unworked – 15 sts (7 dc on each side of corner tr).

Row 4: Ch 1, turn, sc in each st to corner tr, (sc, hdc, sc) in corner tr, sc in each st across – 17 sts (8 sc on each side of corner hdc).

Row 5: Ch 3 (counts as dc), turn, dc in each st to corner hdc, (2 dc, tr, 2 dc) in corner hdc, dc in each st across and change to D in last st – 21 sts (10 dc on each side of corner tr).

Rows 6-9: Rep Rows 4 and 5 twice, working Rows 6 and 7 with D and Rows 8 and 9 with E – 33 sts (16 dc on each side of corner tr) at the end of Row 9.
Fasten off.

MITERED SQUARE II
(make 8)

Make same as Mitered Square I, working Rnds 1 and 2 with A, Rows 3 and 4 with F, Row 5 with D, Rows 6 and 7 with C, and Rows 8 and 9 with B.

MITERED SQUARE III
(make 6)

Make same as Mitered Square I, working Rnds 1 and 2 with A, Rows 3 and 4 with B, Rows 5 and 6 with D, Row 7 with E, and Rows 8 and 9 with F.

MITERED SQUARE IV
(make 4)

Make same as Mitered Square I, working Rnds 1 and 2 with A, Rows 3 and 4 with B, Rows 5-7 with C, and Rows 8 and 9 with F.

FINISHING

Sew Squares together following diagram.

Border

From RS, join C with sl st anywhere along outside edge of Afghan.

Rnd 1 (RS): Ch 1, sc evenly spaced all the way around outside edge, working (sc, hdc, sc) in each outer corner; join with sl st in first sc.

Note: To work evenly around outer edge, we suggest working 15 sc along each short edge (sides of Mitered Squares and partial sides of Large Squares) and 65 sc along each long edge (side edge of 2 neighboring Large Squares), and skipping the inner corners (valleys).

Rnd 2: Ch 2 (counts as hdc), turn, hdc in each st around working (hdc, dc, hdc) in hdc at each outer corner and skipping the 2 sts at each inner corner; join with sl st in top of beg ch. Fasten off.

Weave in ends.

COLOR KEY

- #100 White (A)
- #153 Black (B)
- #151 Charcoal Grey (C)
- #149 Silver Grey (D)
- #405 Silver Heather (E)
- #158 Mustard (F)

SQUARE KEY

- Large Square I
- Large Square II
- Large Square III
- Mitered Square I
- Mitered Square II
- Mitered Square III
- Mitered Square IV

Star Mandala Afghan

INTERMEDIATE

SIZE

About 58" (147.5 cm) diameter

Shopping List

Yarn (Medium Weight) MEDIUM 4

LION BRAND® VANNA'S CHOICE®
(Art. #860)

- ☐ #125 Taupe - 3 balls (A)
- ☐ #123 Beige - 1 ball (B)
- ☐ #158 Mustard - 1 ball (C)
- ☐ #135 Rust - 1 ball (D)
- ☐ #176 Peacock - 1 ball (E)
- ☐ #108 Dusty Blue - 1 ball (F)
- ☐ #109 Colonial Blue - 1 ball (G)
- ☐ #105 Silver Blue - 1 ball (H)
- ☐ #106 Aquamarine - 2 balls (I)

or colors of your choice

Crochet Hook

LION BRAND® crochet hook

- ☐ Size I-9 (5.5 mm)

or size needed for gauge

Additional Supplies

- ☐ LION BRAND® stitch markers
- ☐ LION BRAND® large-eyed blunt needle

GAUGE

12 dc and 6 rows/rnds = about 4" (10 cm).
1 Large Square = about 6" x 6" (15 cm x 15 cm).
1 Octagon = about 13½" (34.5 cm) across.
1 Small Square = about 4" x 4" (10 cm x 10 cm).
BE SURE TO CHECK YOUR GAUGE.

TECHNIQUE EXPLANATION

Adjustable Ring Method

Wrap yarn around index finger. Insert hook into ring on finger, yarn over and draw up a loop. Carefully slip ring from finger and work the stitches of Rnd 1 (in pattern, page 32) into the ring. When Rnd 1 is complete, gently but firmly, pull yarn tail to tighten center of ring.

STITCH GUIDE

DOUBLE CROCHET 2 TOGETHER (abbreviated dc2tog)

(Yarn over, insert hook in next st and draw up a loop, yarn over and draw through 2 loops) twice, yarn over and draw through all 3 loops on hook – 1 st decreased.

DOUBLE CROCHET 3 TOGETHER (abbreviated dc3tog)

(Yarn over, insert hook in next st and draw up a loop, yarn over, draw through 2 loops) 3 times, yarn over and draw through all 4 loops on hook – 2 sts decreased.

REVERSE SINGLE CROCHET (abbreviated rev sc)

Single crochet worked from left to right (right to left, if left-handed). Insert hook into next stitch to the right (left), under loop on hook, and draw up a loop. Yarn over and draw through all loops on hook.

SINGLE CROCHET 3 TOGETHER (abbreviated sc3tog)

(Insert hook in next st and draw up a loop) 3 times, yarn over and draw through all 4 loops on hook – 2 sts decreased.

NOTES

1. Afghan is made from 25 pieces: 1 Star, 8 Large Squares, 8 Octagons, and 8 Small Squares.
2. Star is worked in 2 steps. First, the Center is worked in joined rnds with RS always facing, then 8 points are worked back and forth in rows around the outside edge of the Center.
3. Large and Small Squares are worked back and forth in rows to make mitered squares.
4. Octagons are worked in joined rnds with RS always facing.
5. Pieces are sewn together following a diagram.

STAR

Center

Notes:

1. In this section work all rnds with the RS always facing. Do not turn at beginning of rnds.
2. To change yarn color in this section, fasten off old color and join new color as instructed.

With A, ch 4; join with sl st in first ch to form a ring.

Rnd 1 (RS): Ch 3 (counts as first dc), work 11 more dc in ring; join with sl st in top of beg ch – 12 dc. Fasten off.

Rnd 2: From RS, draw up a loop of B in any st, ch 3 (counts as dc), dc in same st, 2 dc in each st around; join with sl st in top of beg ch – 24 dc. Fasten off.

Rnd 3: From RS, draw up a loop of E in any st, ch 3 (counts as dc), 2 dc in next st, *dc in next st, 2 dc in next st; rep from * around; join with sl st in top of beg ch – 36 dc. Fasten off.

Rnd 4: From RS, draw up a loop of F in any st, ch 3 (counts as dc), dc in next st, 2 dc in next st, *dc in next 2 sts, 2 dc in next st; rep from * around; join with sl st in top of beg ch – 48 dc. Fasten off.

Rnd 5: From RS, draw up a loop of B in any st, ch 3 (counts as dc), dc in next 2 sts, 2 dc in next st, *dc in next 3 sts, 2 dc in next st; rep from * around; join with sl st in top of beg ch – 60 dc. Fasten off.

Rnd 6: From RS, draw up a loop of D in any st, ch 3 (counts as dc), dc in next 3 sts, 2 dc in next st, *dc in next 4 sts, 2 dc in next st; rep from * around; join with sl st in top of beg ch – 72 dc. Do not fasten off.

Rnd 7: Ch 3 (counts as dc), dc in next 4 sts, 2 dc in next st, *dc in next 5 sts, 2 dc in next st; rep from * around; join with sl st in top of beg ch – 84 dc. Fasten off.

Rnd 8: From RS, draw up a loop of C in any st, ch 3 (counts as dc), dc in next 5 sts, 2 dc in next st, *dc in next 6 sts, 2 dc in next st; rep from * around; join with sl st in top of beg ch – 96 dc. Fasten off.

Rnd 9: From RS, draw up a loop of F in any st, ch 3 (counts as dc), dc in next 6 sts, 2 dc in next st, *dc in next 7 sts, 2 dc in next st; rep from * around; join with sl st in top of beg ch – 108 dc. Fasten off.

Rnd 10: From RS, draw up a loop of B in any st, ch 3 (counts as dc), dc in next 7 sts, 2 dc in next st, *dc in next 8 sts, 2 dc in next st; rep from * around; join with sl st in top of beg ch – 120 dc. Fasten off.

Rnd 11: From RS, draw up a loop of D in any st, ch 3 (counts as dc), dc in next 8 sts, 2 dc in next st, *dc in next 9 sts, 2 dc in next st; rep from * around; join with sl st in top of beg ch – 132 dc. Fasten off.

Rnd 12: From RS, join A with sc in any st, sc in next 31 sts, 2 sc in next st, *sc in next 32 sts, 2 sc in next st; rep from * around; join with sl st in first sc – 136 sc. Fasten off.

Points

To change yarn color, work last st of old color to last yarn over. Yarn over with new color and draw through all loops on hook to complete st. Proceed with new color. Cut old color.

Place a marker in any st of last rnd, *skip the next 16 sts, place a marker in the next st; rep from * until a total of 8 markers have been placed, with 16 sts between marked sts. Your work is now divided into 8 sections of 17 sts each. A point will be worked over each of these 8 sections.

Row 1 (WS): From WS, join E with sl st in any marked st, ch 3 (counts as dc), dc in next 16 sts; leave remaining sts unworked – 17 dc.

Rows 2 and 3: Ch 3 (counts as dc), turn, dc2tog, dc in each st to last 3 sts, dc2tog, dc in top of beg ch and change to F in last st of Row 3 – 13 dc at the end of Row 3.

Rows 4 and 5: With F, rep Rows 2 and 3 and change to B in last st of Row 5 – 9 dc at the end of Row 5.

Row 6: With B, rep Row 2 and change to A in last st – 7 dc.

Row 7: With A, rep Row 2 and change to D in last st – 5 dc.

Row 8: With D, ch 3 (counts as dc), turn, dc3tog, dc in top of beg ch – 3 dc.

Row 9: With D, ch 1, turn, sc3tog. Fasten off.

Rep Rows 1-9 beg at each marked st until all 8 points have been completed.
Remove markers.

LARGE SQUARE (make 8)

When working Large Squares, change yarn color same as for Star-Points.

With E, make an adjustable ring.

Row 1: Ch 3 (counts as dc), (dc, ch 2, 2 dc) in ring – 4 dc and 1 ch-2 sp (2 dc on each side of ch-2 sp).

Row 2: Ch 3 (counts as dc), turn, dc in next st, (2 dc, ch 2, 2 dc) in ch-2 sp, dc in next st, dc in top of beg ch – 8 dc and 1 center ch-2 sp (4 dc on each side of center ch-2 sp).

Row 3: Ch 3 (counts as dc), turn, dc in each st to center ch-2 sp, (2 dc, ch 2, 2 dc) in ch-2 sp, dc in each st to end working last dc in top of beg ch and change to F in last st – 12 dc and 1 center ch-2 sp (6 dc on each side of center ch-2 sp).

Rows 4 and 5: With F, rep Row 3 twice and change color to B in last st of Row 5 – 20 dc and 1 center ch-2 sp at the end of Row 5 (10 dc on each side of center ch-2 sp) at the end of Row 5.

Row 6: With B, rep Row 3 and change to A in last st – 24 dc and 1 center ch-2 sp (12 dc on each side of center ch-2 sp).

Row 7: With A, rep Row 3 and change to D in last st – 28 dc and 1 center ch-2 sp (14 dc on each side of center ch-2 sp).

Rows 8 and 9: With D, rep Row 3 twice, do not change color – 36 dc and 1 center ch-2 sp (18 dc on each side of center ch-2 sp) at the end of Row 9.
Fasten off.

OCTAGON (make 8)

Work in joined rnds, changing yarn color same as for Star-Center.

With A, ch 4; join with sl st in first ch to form a ring.

Rnds 1-10: Work same as Rnds 1-10 of Star using the following colors: Work Rnd 1 with G, Rnd 2 with H, Rnd 3 with F, Rnds 4 and 5 with G, Rnd 6 with B, Rnd 7 with C, Rnd 8 with A, Rnd 9 with H, Rnd 10 with I – 120 dc at the end of Rnd 10.
Do NOT fasten off at the end of Rnd 10.

Rnd 11: With I, ch 3 (counts as dc), dc in next 13 sts, (dc, ch 2, dc) in next st, *dc in next 14 sts, (dc, ch 2, dc) in next st; rep from * around; join with sl st in top of beg ch – 128 dc and 8 ch-2 sps (16 dc between ch-2 sps).
Fasten off.

Rnd 12: From RS, join E with sc in any st, sc in each st around working 3 sc in each ch-2 sp; join with sl st in first sc – 152 sc.
Fasten off.

Rnd 13: From RS, draw up a loop of A in 3rd sc of any 3-sc group, ch 3 (counts as dc), *dc in each st to center sc of next 3-sc group, (dc, ch 2, dc) in center sc of 3-sc group; rep from * around; join with sl st in top of beg ch – 160 dc and 8 ch-2 sps (20 dc between ch-2 sps).
Fasten off.

SMALL SQUARE (make 8)

Small Squares are all worked with A.

With A, make an adjustable ring as for Large Square.

Rows 1-6: Working with A only, work same as Rows 1-6 of Large Square – 24 dc and 1 center ch-2 sp (12 dc on each side of center ch-2 sp) at the end of Row 6.
Fasten off.

FINISHING

Following diagram,

1. Sew 2 sides of each Large Square into the spaces between points.
2. Sew Octagons together into a ring.
3. Sew ring of Octagons to Large Squares.
4 Sew 2 sides of each Small Square into the spaces between Octagons.

Border

From RS, draw up a loop of A in any stitch along outside edge of Afghan. Ch 1, work rev sc evenly spaced around entire outside edge of Afghan, working 2 rev sc in each ch-2 sp; join with sl st in beg ch.
Fasten off.

Weave in ends.

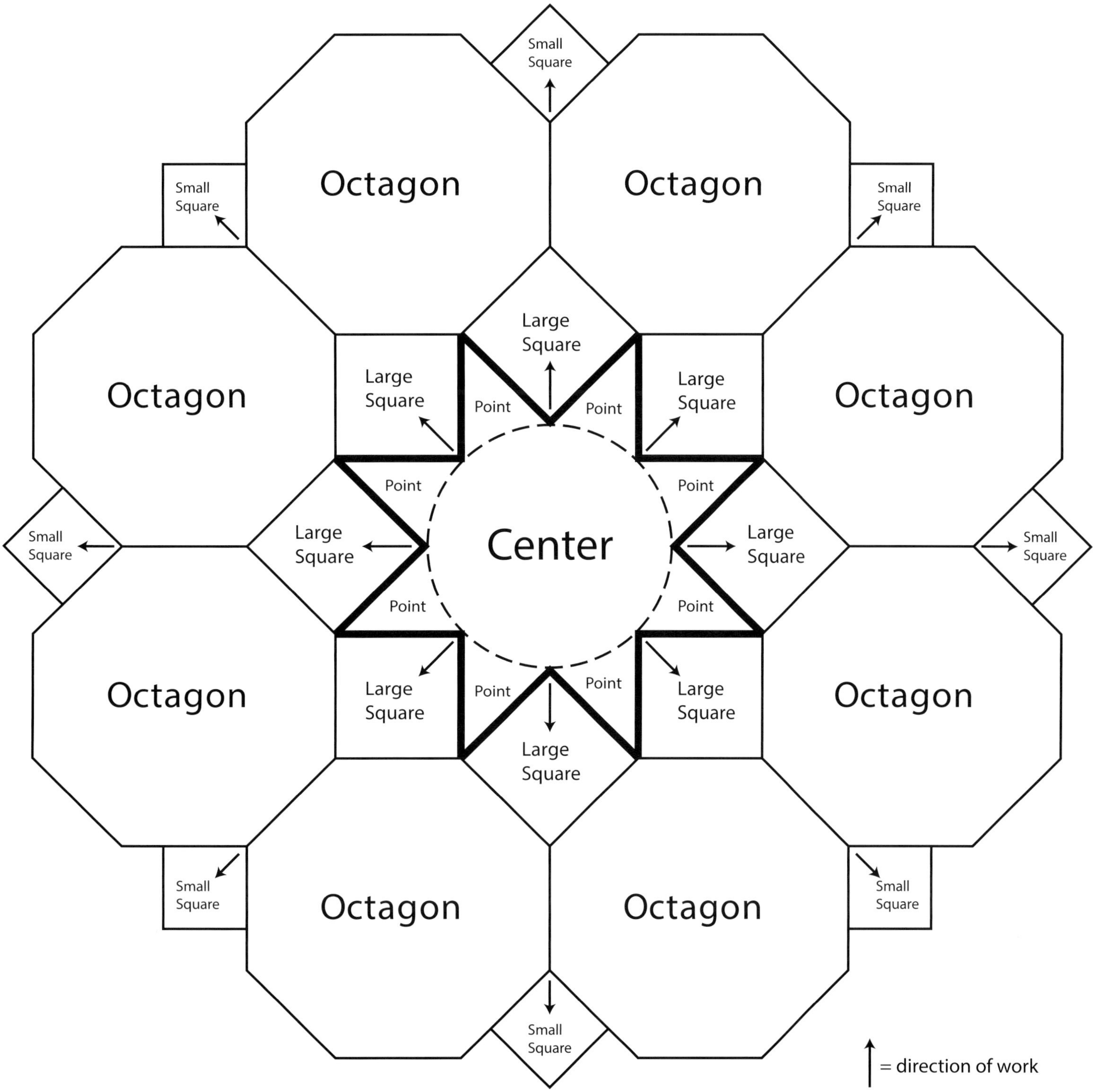
Small Square
Octagon
Octagon
Small Square
Small Square
Large Square
Octagon
Large Square
Large Square
Octagon
Point
Point
Point
Point
Small Square
Large Square
Center
Large Square
Small Square
Point
Point
Octagon
Large Square
Point
Point
Large Square
Octagon
Large Square
Small Square
Octagon
Octagon
Small Square
Small Square
= direction of work

Sea Salt Circle Afghan

EASY +

SIZES

About 50" (127 cm) diameter

Shopping List

Yarn (Medium Weight) MEDIUM 4

LION BRAND® VANNA'S CHOICE® (Art. #860)

- ☐ #099 Linen - 1 ball (A)
- ☐ #125 Taupe - 1 ball (B)
- ☐ #400 Oatmeal - 2 balls (C)
- ☐ #406 Obsidian - 1 ball (D)
- ☐ #123 Beige - 1 ball (E)
- ☐ #149 Silver Grey - 1 ball (F)
- ☐ #401 Grey Marble - 1 ball (G)
- ☐ #151 Charcoal Grey - 1 ball (H)

or colors of your choice

Crochet Hook

LION BRAND® crochet hook

- ☐ Size K-10.5 (6.5 mm)

or size needed for gauge

Additional Supply

- ☐ LION BRAND® large-eyed blunt needle

GAUGE

Rnds 1-3 = about 4" (10 cm) in diameter circle.

BE SURE TO CHECK YOUR GAUGE.

STITCH GUIDE

BEGINNING 2 DOUBLE CROCHET CLUSTER (abbreviated beg 2-dc Cl)

Ch 3, yarn over, insert hook in indicated st and draw up a loop, yarn over and draw through 2 loops on hook (2 loops rem on hook); yarn over and draw through rem 2 loops on hook.

2 DOUBLE CROCHET CLUSTER (abbreviated 2-dc Cl)

Yarn over, insert hook in indicated st and draw up a loop, yarn over and draw through 2 loops on hook (2 loops rem on hook), yarn over, insert hook in *same* st and draw up a loop, yarn over and draw through 2 loops on hook, yarn over and draw through all 3 loops on hook.

BEGINNING 3 DOUBLE CROCHET CLUSTER (abbreviated beg 3-dc Cl)

Ch 3, yarn over, insert hook in indicated st and draw up a loop, yarn over and draw through 2 loops on hook (2 loops rem on hook); yarn over, insert hook in *same* st and draw up a loop, yarn over and draw through 2 loops on hook, yarn over and draw through all 3 loops on hook.

3 DOUBLE CROCHET CLUSTER (abbreviated 3-dc Cl)

Yarn over, insert hook in indicated st, yarn over and draw up a loop, yarn over and draw through 2 loops on hook (2 loops rem on hook), (yarn over, insert hook in *same* st, yarn over and draw up a loop, yarn over and draw through 2 loops on hook) twice; yarn over and draw through all 4 loops on hook.

REVERSE SINGLE CROCHET (abbreviated rev sc)

Single crochet worked from left to right (right to left, if left-handed). Insert hook into next stitch to the right (left), under loop on hook, and draw up a loop. Yarn over and draw through all loops on hook.

NOTES

1. Afghan is worked in one piece in joined rnds with RS always facing. Do not turn at beg of rnds.
2. To change yarn color, fasten off old color and join new color as instructed.

AFGHAN

With A, ch 6; join with sl st in first ch to form a ring.

Rnd 1 (RS): Ch 3 (counts as first dc), work 11 more dc in ring; join with sl st in top of beg ch – 12 dc. Fasten off.

Rnd 2: From RS, join B with sc in any sp between sts, *ch 1, sc in next sp between sts; rep from * around, ch 1; join with sl st in first sc – 12 sc and 12 ch-1 sps. Fasten off.

Rnd 3: From RS, draw up a loop of C in any ch-1 sp, beg 3-dc Cl in same ch-1 sp, *ch 2, 3-dc Cl in next ch-1 sp; rep from * around, ch 2; join with sl st in top of beg 3-dc Cl – 12 Cl and 12 ch-2 sps. Fasten off.

Rnd 4: From RS, draw up a loop of D in any ch-2 sp, (beg 2-dc Cl, ch 1, 2-dc Cl) in same ch-2 sp, *ch 1, (2-dc Cl, ch 1, 2-dc Cl) in next ch-2 sp; rep from * around, ch 1; join with sl st in top of beg 2-dc Cl – 24 Cl and 24 ch-1 sps. Fasten off.

Rnd 5: From RS, join E with sc in any ch-1 sp, sc in same ch-1 sp, *ch 1, 2 sc in next ch-1 sp; rep from * around, ch 1; join with sl st in first sc – 48 sc and 24 ch-1 sps. Fasten off.

Rnd 6: From RS, draw up a loop of B in any ch-1 sp, ch 3 (counts as dc), 2 dc in same ch-1 sp, 3 dc in each rem ch-1 sp around; join with sl st in top of beg ch – Twenty-four 3-dc groups. Fasten off.

Rnd 7: From RS, join A with sc in any st, *ch 1, sk next st, sc in next st; rep from * to last st, ch 1, sk last st; join with sl st in first sc – 36 sc and 36 ch-1 sps. Do not fasten off.

Rnd 8: With A, (sl st, beg 3-dc Cl) in first ch-1 sp, *ch 2, 3-dc Cl in next ch-1 sp; rep from * around, ch 2; join with sl st in top of beg 3-dc Cl – 36 Cl and 36 ch-2 sps. Fasten off.

Rnd 9: From RS, draw up a loop of F in any ch-2 sp, (beg 2-dc Cl, ch 1, 2-dc Cl) in same ch-2 sp, ch 1, 2-dc Cl in next ch-2 sp, *ch 1, (2-dc Cl, ch 1, 2-dc Cl) in next ch-2 sp, ch 1, 2-dc Cl in next ch-2 sp; rep from * around, ch 1; join with sl st in top of beg 2-dc Cl – 54 Cl and 54 ch-1 sps. Fasten off.

Rnd 10: From RS, join G with sc in any ch-1 sp, sc in same ch-1 sp, 2 sc in each rem ch-1 sp around; join with sl st in first sc – Fifty-four 2-sc groups. Fasten off.

Rnd 11: From RS, draw up a loop of H in any sp between 2-sc groups, ch 3 (counts as dc), dc in same sp, 2 dc in each rem sp between 2-sc groups; join with sl st in top of beg ch – Fifty-four 2-dc groups. Fasten off.

Rnd 12: From RS, join C with sc in any st, *ch 1, sk next st, sc in next st; rep from * to last st, ch 1, sk last st; join with sl st in first sc – 54 sc and 54 ch-1 sps. Fasten off.

Rnd 13: From RS, draw up a loop of E in any ch-1 sp, beg 3-dc Cl in same ch-1 sp, *ch 2, 3-dc Cl in next ch-1 sp; rep from * around, ch 2; join with sl st in top of beg 3-dc Cl – 54 Cl and 54 ch-2 sps. Fasten off.

Rnd 14: From RS, draw up a loop of C in any ch-2 sp, (beg 2-dc Cl, ch 1, 2-dc Cl) in same ch-2 sp, (ch 1, 2-dc Cl in next ch-2 sp) twice, *ch 1, (2-dc Cl, ch 1, 2-dc Cl) in next ch-2 sp, (ch 1, 2-dc Cl in next ch-2 sp) twice; rep from * around, ch 1; join with sl st in top of beg 2-dc Cl – 72 Cl and 72 ch-1 sps. Fasten off.

Rnd 15: With B, rep Rnd 10 – 72 sc-groups. Fasten off.

Rnd 16: With D, rep Rnd 11 – 72 dc-groups. Fasten off.

Rnd 17: With H, rep Rnd 12 – 72 sc and 72 ch-1 sps. Fasten off.

Rnd 18: With G, rep Rnd 13 – 72 Cl and 72 ch-2 sps. Fasten off.

Rnd 19: From RS, draw up a loop of H in any ch-2 sp, (beg 2-dc Cl, ch 1, 2-dc Cl) in same ch-2 sp, (ch 1, 2-dc Cl in next ch-2 sp) 3 times, *ch 1, (2-dc Cl, ch 1, 2-dc Cl) in next ch-2 sp, (ch 1, 2-dc Cl in next ch-2 sp) 3 times; rep from * around, ch 1; join with sl st in top of beg 2-dc Cl – 90 Cl and 90 ch-1 sps. Fasten off.

Rnd 20: With F, rep Rnd 10 – 90 sc-groups. Fasten off.

Rnd 21: With A, rep Rnd 11 – 90 dc-groups. Fasten off.

Rnd 22: With B, rep Rnd 12 – 90 sc and 90 ch-1 sps. Fasten off.

Rnd 23: With C, rep Rnd 13 – 90 Cl and 90 ch-2 sps. Fasten off.

Rnd 24: From RS, draw up a loop of B in any ch-2 sp, (beg 2-dc Cl, ch 1, 2-dc Cl) in same ch-2 sp, (ch 1, 2-dc Cl in next ch-2 sp) 4 times, *ch 1, (2-dc Cl, ch 1, 2-dc Cl) in next ch-2 sp, (ch 1, 2-dc Cl in next ch-2 sp) 4 times; rep from * around, ch 1; join with sl st in top of beg 2-dc Cl – 108 Cl and 108 ch-1 sps. Fasten off.

Rnd 25: With D, rep Rnd 10 – 108 sc-groups. Fasten off.

Rnd 26: With E, rep Rnd 11 – 108 dc-groups. Fasten off.

Rnd 27: With A, rep Rnd 12 – 108 sc and 108 ch-1 sps. Fasten off.

Rnd 28: With F, rep Rnd 13 – 108 Cl and 108 ch-2 sps. Fasten off.

Rnd 29: From RS, draw up a loop of A in any ch-2 sp, (beg 2-dc Cl, ch 1, 2-dc Cl) in same ch-2 sp, (ch 1, 2-dc Cl in next ch-2 sp) 5 times, *ch 1, (2-dc Cl, ch 1, 2-dc Cl) in next ch-2 sp, (ch 1, 2-dc Cl in next ch-2 sp) 5 times; rep from * around, ch 1; join with sl st in top of beg 2-dc Cl – 126 Cl and 126 ch-1 sps. Fasten off.

Rnd 30: With H, rep Rnd 10 – 126 sc-groups. Fasten off.

Rnd 31: With G, rep Rnd 11 – 126 dc-groups. Fasten off.

Rnd 32: With E, rep Rnd 12 – 126 sc and 126 ch-1 sps. Fasten off.

Rnd 33: With D, rep Rnd 13 – 126 Cl and 126 ch-2 sps. Fasten off.

Rnd 34: From RS, draw up a loop of E in any ch-2 sp, (beg 2-dc Cl, ch 1, 2-dc Cl) in same ch-2 sp, (ch 1, 2-dc Cl in next ch-2 sp) 6 times, *ch 1, (2-dc Cl, ch 1, 2-dc Cl) in next ch-2 sp, (ch 1, 2-dc Cl in next ch-2 sp) 6 times; rep from * around, ch 1; join with sl st in top of beg 2-dc Cl – 144 Cl and 144 ch-1 sps. Fasten off.

Rnd 35: With C, rep Rnd 10 – 144 sc-groups. Fasten off.

Rnd 36: With B, rep Rnd 11 – 144 dc-groups. Fasten off.

Rnd 37: With H, rep Rnd 12 – 144 sc and 144 ch-1 sps. Fasten off.

Rnd 38: With C, rep Rnd 13 – 144 Cl and 144 ch-2 sps. Fasten off.

Rnd 39: From RS, draw up a loop of H in any ch-2 sp, (beg 2-dc Cl, ch 1, 2-dc Cl) in same ch-2 sp, (ch 1, 2-dc Cl in next ch-2 sp) 3 times, *ch 1, (2-dc Cl, ch 1, 2-dc Cl) in next ch-2 sp, (ch 1, 2-dc Cl in next ch-2 sp) 3 times; rep from * around, ch 1; join with sl st in top of beg 2-dc Cl – 180 Cl and 180 ch-1 sps. Fasten off.

Rnd 40: With G, rep Rnd 10 – 180 sc-groups. Fasten off.

Rnd 41: With F, rep Rnd 11 – 180 dc-groups. Fasten off.

Rnd 42: With A, rep Rnd 12 – 180 sc and 180 ch-1 sps. Fasten off.

Rnd 43: With C, rep Rnd 13 – 180 Cl and 180 ch-2 sps. Fasten off.

Rnd 44: From RS, join A with sc in any ch-2 sp, sc in same ch-2 sp, *ch 1, 2 sc in next ch-2 sp; rep from * around, ch 1; join with sl st in first sc – 180 sc-groups and 180 ch-1 sps. Fasten off.

Rnd 45: From RS, draw up a loop of B in any ch-1 sp, ch 1, rev sc in same ch-1 sp, *ch 3, rev sc in next ch-1 sp; rep from * around; join with sl st in beg ch – 180 rev sc and 180 ch-3 sps. Fasten off.

FINISHING

Weave in ends.

Pine Bluff Mandala Afghan

EASY

Shown on page 42.

SIZE

About 39" x 39" (99 cm x 99 cm), not including edging

Shopping List

Yarn (Medium Weight) MEDIUM 4

LION BRAND® VANNA'S CHOICE® (Art. #860)

- ☐ #100 White - 1 ball (A)
- ☐ #139 Rose Shocking -2 balls (B)
- ☐ #158 Mustard - 1 ball (C)
- ☐ #405 Silver Heather - 1 ball (D)
- ☐ #153 Black - 4 balls (E)

or colors of your choice

Crochet Hook

LION BRAND® crochet hook

- ☐ Size J-10 (6 mm)

or size needed for gauge

Additional Supply

- ☐ LION BRAND® large-eyed blunt needle

GAUGE

1 Square = about 13" x 13" (33 cm x 33 cm).

BE SURE TO CHECK YOUR GAUGE.

STITCH GUIDE

DOUBLE TREBLE/TRIPLE CROCHET (abbreviated dtr)

(Yarn over) 3 times, insert hook in indicated st and draw up a loop, (yarn over and draw through 2 loops on hook) 4 times.

NOTES

1. 9 Squares are worked separately, then sewn together to make the Afghan.
2. Yarn color is changed by fastening off the old color and joining the new color.
3. An edging is worked around the outside edge of the Afghan.

SQUARE I (make 5)

With A, ch 4; join with sl st in first ch to form a ring.

Rnd 1 (RS): Ch 3 (counts as dc), dc in ring, (ch 2, 2 dc in ring) 5 times, ch 2; join with sl st in top of beg ch – six 2-dc groups and 6 ch-2 sps .

Rnd 2: Sl st in next dc, sl st in first ch-2 sp, ch 3 (counts as dc), (dc, ch 1, 2 dc) in same ch-2 sp, *ch 1, (2 dc, ch 1, 2 dc) in next ch-2 sp; rep from * around, ch 1; join with sl st in top of beg ch – Twelve 2-dc groups and 12 ch-1 sps.

Fasten off.

Rnd 3: From RS, draw up a loop of B in any ch-1 sp, ch 3 (counts as dc), 2 dc in same ch-1 sp, *ch 1, 3 dc in next ch-1 sp; rep from * around, ch 1; join with sl st in top of beg ch – Twelve 3-dc groups and 12 ch-1 sps.

Rnd 4: Sl st in next 2 dc, sl st in first ch-1 sp, ch 3 (counts as dc), (dc, ch 1, 2 dc) in same ch-1 sp, *ch 1, (2 dc, ch 1, 2 dc) in next ch-1 sp; rep from * around, ch 1; join with sl st in top of beg ch – Twenty-four 2-dc groups and 24 ch-1 sps.

Rnd 5: Sl st in next dc, sl st in first ch-1 sp, ch 3 (counts as dc), 2 dc in same ch-1 sp, *ch 1, 3 dc in next ch-1 sp; rep from * around, ch 1; join with sl st in top of beg ch – Twenty-four 3-dc groups and 24 ch-1 sps.

Rnd 6: Sl st in next 2 dc, sl st in first ch-1 sp, ch 3 (counts as dc), 2 dc in same ch-1 sp, *ch 2, 3 dc in next ch-1 sp; rep from * around, ch 2; join with sl st in top of beg ch – Twenty-four 3-dc groups and 24 ch-2 sps.
Fasten off.

Rnd 7: From RS, draw up a loop of D in any ch-2 sp, ch 3 (counts as dc), (dc, ch 1, 2 dc) in same ch-2 sp, ch 1, 3 dc in next ch-2 sp, *ch 1, (2 dc, ch 1, 2 dc) in next ch-2 sp, ch 1, 3 dc in next ch-2 sp; rep from * around, ch 1; join with sl st in top of beg ch – Twenty-four 2-dc groups, twelve 3-dc groups and 36 ch-1 sps. Fasten off.

Rnd 8: From RS, join E with sc in any ch-1 sp, 2 sc in same ch-1 sp, ch 1, 3 hdc in next ch-1 sp, ch 1, 3 dc in next ch-1 sp, ch 1, 3 tr in next ch-1 sp, ch 1, 3 dtr in next ch-1 sp, ch 3 (corner made), 3 dtr in next ch-1 sp, ch 1, 3 tr in next ch-1 sp, ch 1, 3 dc in next ch-1 sp, ch 1, 3 hdc in next ch-1 sp, *ch 1, 3 sc in next ch-1 sp, ch 1, 3 hdc in next ch-1 sp, ch 1, 3 dc in next ch-1 sp, ch 1, 3 tr in next ch-1 sp, ch 1, 3 dtr in next ch-1 sp, ch 3 (corner made), 3 dtr in next ch-1 sp, ch 1, 3 tr in next ch-1 sp, ch 1, 3 dc in next ch-1 sp, ch 1, 3 hdc in next ch-1 sp; rep from * around, ch 1; join with sl st in first sc – 108 sts and 36 ch-sps (27 sts across each of 4 sides between ch-3 corner sps).

Rnd 9: Sl st in next 2 sc, sl st in first ch-1 sp, ch 3 (counts as dc), 2 dc in same ch-1 sp, (ch 1, 3 dc in next ch-1 sp) 3 times, ch 1, (3 dc, ch 3, 3 dc) in corner ch-3 sp, *(ch 1, 3 dc in next ch-1 sp) 8 times, ch 1, (3 dc, ch 3, 3 dc) in corner ch-3 sp; rep from * to last 4 ch-1 sps, (ch 1, 3 dc in next ch-1 sp) 4 times, ch 1; join with sl st in top of beg ch – Forty 3-dc groups and 40 ch-sps.
Fasten off.

SQUARE II (make 4)

Make same as Square I working Rnds 1 and 2 with A, Rnds 3-6 with C, Rnd 7 with D, and Rnds 8 and 9 with E.

FINISHING

Sew Squares into 3 Strips in the following order:
Strip #1: Square I, Square II, Square I.
Strip #2: Square II, Square I, Square II.
Strip #3: Square I, Square II, Square I.
Sew long edges of Strips tog in following order: Strip #1, Strip #2, Strip #3.

Edging

Rnd 1 (RS): From RS, join E with sl st in any corner ch-3 sp, ch 1, beg in same corner ch-3 sp, **5 sc in corner ch-3 sp, *(ch 3, sc in next ch-1 sp) to ch-sp before seam between Squares, ch 3, sc in corner ch-sp of Square before seam, sc in corner ch-sp of next Square following seam; rep from * once more, (ch 3, sc in next ch-1 sp) to ch-3 sp at next corner of Afghan, ch 3; rep from ** 3 more times; join with sl st in first sc.

Rnd 2 (WS): Ch 3 (counts as dc), turn, 3 dc in each ch-3 sp and dc in each st around working 3 dc in center sc of each 5-sc corner; join with sl st in top of beg ch.

Rnd 3 (WS): Ch 1, do NOT turn, sc in each st around working 3 sc in center dc of each 3-dc corner; join with sl st in first sc.
Fasten off.

Weave in ends.

Wheel of Fortune Mandala Afghan

EASY

SIZE

About 30" x 65" (76 cm x 165 cm) at widest and longest

Shopping List

Yarn (Medium Weight) MEDIUM 4

LION BRAND® VANNA'S CHOICE® (Art. #860)

- ☐ #098 Fisherman - 1 ball (A)
- ☐ #139 Rose Shocking - 1 ball (B)
- ☐ #101 Pink - 1 ball (C)
- ☐ #301 Rose Mist - 1 ball (D)
- ☐ #303 Purple Mist - 1 ball (E)
- ☐ #104 Pink Grapefruit - 1 ball (F)
- ☐ #304 Seaspray Mist - 1 ball (G)
- ☐ #176 Peacock - 1 ball (H)
- ☐ #171 Fern - 1 ball (I)
- ☐ #108 Dusty Blue - 1 ball (J)
- ☐ #106 Aquamarine - 1 ball (K)
- ☐ #300 Denim Mist - 1 ball (L)
- ☐ #111 Sky Blue - 1 ball (M)
- ☐ #105 Silver Blue - 1 ball (N)
- ☐ #102 Aqua - 1 ball (O)

or colors of your choice

Crochet Hook

LION BRAND® crochet hook

- ☐ Size J-10 (6 mm)

or size needed for gauge

Additional Supply

- ☐ LION BRAND® large-eyed blunt needle

GAUGE

1 Triangle = about 6" (15 cm) from point to point

BE SURE TO CHECK YOUR GAUGE.

TECHNIQUE EXPLANATION

Adjustable Ring Method

Wrap yarn around index finger. Insert hook into ring on finger, yarn over and draw up a loop. Carefully slip ring from finger and work the stitches of Rnd 1 (in pattern, below) into the ring. When Rnd 1 is complete, gently but firmly, pull yarn tail to tighten center of ring.

NOTES

1. 78 Triangles are worked separately in rnds with the RS always facing.
2. A stitch diagram is provided to clarify the Triangle.
3. Following a diagram, the Triangles are sewn together in groups of 6 to make hexagons, then the hexagons are sewn together to make the Afghan.
4. Circles are worked separately, then sewn to Afghan. These circles will fill in the gaps between Triangles.

TRIANGLE (make 78: 4 of G; 5 each of D, E, H, I, J and K; 6 each of C, L, M, N and O; 7 each of B and F)

Make an adjustable ring.

Rnd 1 (RS): Ch 8 (counts as first dc, ch 5), (3 dc in ring, ch 5) twice, 2 dc in ring; join with sl st in 3rd ch of beg ch-8 – three 3-dc groups and 3 ch-5 sps.

Rnd 2: Ch 3 (counts as dc), (3 dc, ch 5, 3 dc) in first ch-5 sp, *dc in next 3 dc, (3 dc, ch 5, 3 dc) in next ch-5 sp; rep from * once more, dc in last 2 dc, join with sl st in top of beg ch – 27 dc and 3 ch-5 sps (9 dc across each of 3 sides between corner ch-5 sps).

Rnd 3: Ch 3 (counts as dc), *dc in each st to next ch-5 sp, (3 dc, ch 5, 3 dc) in next ch-5 sp; rep from * 2 more times, dc in each st to end of rnd; join with sl st in top of beg ch – 45 dc and 3 ch-5 sps (15 dc across each of 3 sides between corner ch-5 sps).

Rnd 4: Ch 1, *sc in each dc to next ch-5 sp, 7 sc in next ch-5 sp; rep from * 2 more times, sc in each dc to end of rnd, join with sl st in first sc – 66 sc. Fasten off, leaving a long yarn tail for sewing.

FINISHING

Following diagram, sew Triangles together in groups of 6 to make 13 hexagons, then sew hexagons together to make Afghan.

Center Circle (make 27)

With A, make an adjustable ring. Ch 3, work 11 dc into ring, join with sl st in top of beg ch-3. Fasten off and cut yarn, leaving a long yarn tail.

Following diagram, sew Circles to Afghan.

Weave in ends.

KEY

#098 Fisherman (A)	#107 Peacock (H)
#139 Rose Shocking (B)	#171 Fern (I)
#101 Pink (C)	#108 Dusty Blue (J)
#301 Rose Mist (D)	#106 Aquamarine (K)
#303 Purple Mist (E)	#300 Denim Mist (L)
#104 Pink Grapefruit (F)	#111 Sky Blue (M)
#304 Seaspray (G)	#105 Silver Blue (N)
	#102 Aqua (O)

Triangle

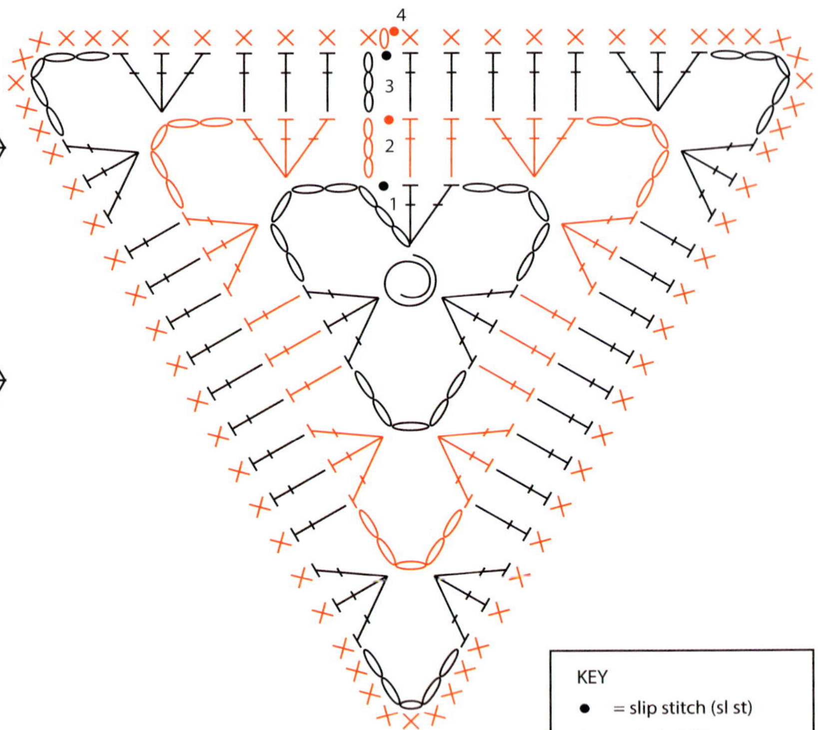

KEY

- ● = slip stitch (sl st)
- ⬭ = chain (ch)
- ✕ = single crochet (sc)
- ⊤ = double crochet (dc)
- ◎ = adjustable ring

General Instructions

ABBREVIATIONS

beg = begin(ning)(s)
ch = chain
ch-sp(s) = chain space(s) previously made
cm = centimeter
dc = double crochet
dtr = double treble/triple crochet
hdc = half double crochet
mm = millimeters
rem = remain(ing)(s)
rep(s) = repeat(s)
RS = right side
rnd(s) = round(s)
sc = single crochet
sk = skip
sl st = slip stitch
sp(s) = space(s)
st(s) = stitch(es)
tog = together
tr = treble (triple) crochet
WS = wrong side

* — When you see an asterisk used within a pattern row, the symbol indicates that later you will be told to repeat a portion of the instruction. Most often the instructions will say, repeat from * so many times.

( ) or **[ ]** — Sets off a short number of stitches that are repeated or indicates additional information.

– When you see – (dash) followed by a number of stitches, this tells you how many stitches you will have at the end of a row or round.

BEGINNER	Projects for first-time crocheters using basic stitches. Minimal shaping.
EASY	Projects using yarn with basic stitches, repetitive stitch patterns, simple color changes, and simple shaping and finishing.
INTERMEDIATE	Projects using a variety of techniques, such as basic lace patterns or color patterns, mid-level shaping and finishing.
EXPERIENCED	Projects with intricate stitch patterns, techniques and dimension, such as non-repeating patterns, multi-color techniques, fine threads, small hooks, detailed shaping and refined finishing.

CROCHET TERMINOLOGY		
UNITED STATES		INTERNATIONAL
slip stitch (slip st)	=	single crochet (sc)
single crochet (sc)	=	double crochet (dc)
half double crochet (hdc)	=	half treble crochet (htr)
double crochet (dc)	=	treble crochet (tr)
treble crochet (tr)	=	double treble crochet (dtr)
double treble crochet (dtr)	=	triple treble crochet (ttr)
triple treble crochet (tr tr)	=	quadruple treble crochet (qtr)
skip	=	miss

Yarn Weight Symbol & Names	LACE 0	SUPER FINE 1	FINE 2	LIGHT 3	MEDIUM 4	BULKY 5	SUPER BULKY 6	JUMBO 7
Type of Yarns in Category	Fingering, size 10 crochet thread	Sock, Fingering, Baby	Sport, Baby	DK, Light Worsted	Worsted, Afghan, Aran	Chunky, Craft, Rug	Super Bulky, Roving	Jumbo, Roving
Crochet Gauge* Ranges in Single Crochet to 4" (10 cm)	32-42 sts**	21-32 sts	16-20 sts	12-17 sts	11-14 sts	8-11 sts	6-9 sts	5 sts and fewer
Advised Hook Size Range	Steel*** 6 to 8, Regular hook B-1	B-1 to E-4	E-4 to 7	7 to I-9	I-9 to K-10½	K-10½ to M/N-13	M/N-13 to Q	Q and larger

*GUIDELINES ONLY: The chart above reflects the most commonly used gauges and hook sizes for specific yarn categories.

** Lace weight yarns are usually crocheted with larger hooks to create lacy openwork patterns. Accordingly, a gauge range is difficult to determine. Always follow the gauge stated in your pattern.

*** Steel crochet hooks are sized differently from regular hooks–the higher the number, the smaller the hook, which is the reverse of regular hook sizing.

CROCHET HOOKS																	
U.S.	B-1	C-2	D-3	E-4	F-5	G-6	7	H-8	I-9	J-10	K-10½	L-11	M/N-13	N/P-15	P/Q	Q	S
Metric - mm	2.25	2.75	3.25	3.5	3.75	4	4.5	5	5.5	6	6.5	8	9	10	15	16	19

GAUGE

Never underestimate the importance of gauge. Achieving the correct gauge assures that the finished size of your piece matches the finished size given in the pattern.

CHECKING YOUR GAUGE

Work a swatch that is at least 4" (10 cm) square. Use the suggested hook size and the number of stitches given. If your swatch is larger than 4" (10 cm), you need to work it again using a smaller hook; if it is smaller than 4" (10 cm), try it with a larger hook. This might require a swatch or two to get the exact gauge given in the pattern.

METRICS

As a handy reference, keep in mind that 1 ounce = approximately 28 grams and 1" = 2.5 centimeters.

TERMS

fasten off — To end your piece, you need to simply cut and pull the yarn through the last loop left on the hook. This keeps the last stitch intact and prevents the work from unraveling.

right side — Refers to the front of the piece.

LION BRAND® VANNA'S CHOICE®

Article #860

Weight Category: 4 - Medium Weight

Solids: 3.5oz/100g (147yd/134m)

Prints, Mists, Tweeds & Heathers: 3oz/85g (145yd/133m)

Fiber Content: 100% Acrylic

Gauge:

Knit: 16 sts x 22 rows = 4" (10 cm) on size 9 (5.5 mm) needles

Crochet: 12 sc x 15 rows = 4" (10 cm) on J-10 (6 mm) hook

Product Care Instructions: Items made from this yarn may be machine laundered. Any dry cleaning solvent may be safely used. No bleach product may be used. Items may be machine dried. Item may not be smoothed or finished with an iron.

VISIT LionBrand.com FOR:

- Learn to Knit & Crochet Instructions
- Weekly newsletter with articles, tips, and updates
- Store Locator